GIBBERISH

A Bipolar Survival Story

Dear Gwen,
Well its finally
Here, and you were
with me every
step of the way!
Thanks for your
love and encouragment
Love
Scott

Scott James Jordan

To order additional copies of this book, contact:
Xlibris Corporation
1-888-795-4274
www.Xlibris.com
Orders@Xlibris.com
18377

CONTENTS

First and foremost to J. Scott Turton.
Jim Turner , Tony Sampson, Liam Nolan ,
Elliott McEldowney IV, Arthur Sjögren
Kate Hunt, Sewall Whittemore,
Will King, Gary Peterson, Jose Pimentel,
Cindy Rosenbaum, David Eliseo, Dr Leonard Alperts,
Dr. Matthew Ruble, Dr. Ari Kissilenko, Rae Akerly,
Dana Ackerly, Barb Apy, Annie, Mike, Kelly, Matt and Brooke.
Dad and Sue.
Andy Padilla, Rocky Crawford, Dan Hawk, Katherine Rouse,
Gary Benjamin, Pingle, Ron Robin,
Mike and Lucky
William Sayegh, Michael Poniatowski, Dan Cersosimo,
Lisa Kiefer, Erin, Eileen and Jake.

To my Mother , Grandmother and Uncle and
all who suffered as I do.

I attended a Thanksgiving dinner in Pacifica California a few years back at the home of a woman named Terry Lynn Snyder. I was in the throes of a severe mania and though I was not aware of it at the time I was being quite disruptive. "I'm going to write a book about my life and then I'm going to make it into a movie." I kept repeating this over and over to any one of the twenty guests as well as a lot of other things that made little or no sense. Finally my hostess, exasperated by my insane behavior and concerned for her other guest's comfort, decided to intervene. "What are you going to call the book." She said pointedly. "I looked at her with great puzzlement and said calmly for the first time that evening" I don't know?"

"Why don't you call it Gibberish." We both laughed at that. It would take three years before I would realize that the joke was on me.

This book did not turn out the way I intended it to. I originally set out to write a memoir. I thought that would be an easy thing to do. I have been telling my life story to therapists for years so naturally it seemed that putting it on paper would be a cinch. I couldn't have been more wrong. I have a newfound respect for authors everywhere. I have compiled all the attempts that I made to commit my life to paper. There are three separate writings. The first is from 1998. At the end of the writing, I entered the worst phase of mania I have ever experienced. The second writing takes place after I have been out of the hospital for about a year and taking a new drug called Geodon. I also include some shorter writings from this time. The last writing is from this year (2002) and brings you up to the present.

This first writing is from 1998. What you will find here is a condensed version of my life story. I was suffering from an ever-increasing mania. I originally set out to write as a therapy for my own sake. I'm not a medical expert on manic depression; I am a sufferer. So I thought I would invite you into my suffering. Paranoia, grandiosity, and pressured speech are some of the more easily recognizable symptoms of manic depression, In reviewing this section of writing I found quite a bit of evidence of these three symptoms.

SCOTT

I struggled with whether or not to include definitions of Bipolar disorder and its symptoms in this book. Most books with Bipolar disorder in the title do include a definition at some point I wanted to stay away from medical jargon and keep this writing as uncomplicated as possible, yet there was a strong desire to explain my sickness in the clearest terms. If I had to pick out the most difficult part about being manic depressive, it would be how misunderstood an illness it is. "Bipolar" is a term that is tossed around a lot today, and I have sometimes felt that people who have had too much coffee think they are suffering from mania. It is also true that everyone gets depressed. When sick, I have encountered a broad consensus from those around me that I was just behaving badly rather than suffering from an actual brain chemical problem. I realize that I am ranting a little here. Back to the definitions. I believe that the definitions themselves are partly to blame. They are often complicated and leave out a lot of information. With that in mind I decided to take the existing definitions and simplify them to the best of my ability, adding anything that I felt was missing and important, I also polled my manic-depressive friends and asked them for their input. After gleaning all that I could from existing sources, I put my own stamp on the phases of Bipolar disorder and defined them from my own personal experience. I hope that this will help reduce some of the judgement associated with this disorder and help people to better identify the illness when they see it,

What is BiPolar

Bipolar disorder is thought to be caused by a brain chemical imbalance. It is characterized by swings of mood from incredible highs to very depressing lows. There are different stages of the disorder: the manic stage, the depression stage, mixed mania and rapid cycling, A person suffering with the illness might go through one or all of the stages and then experience normal moods. Manic Depression is classified as Bipolar I or Bipolar II. If you suffer from Bipolar I you may experience manic episodes, depression or just manic episodes. With Bipolar II you may have depression as your primary symptom with occasional mild manic episodes. Bipolar II's do not experience full blown manias, "Rapid Cycling" is when you alternate between states at least four times a year. In severe cases rapid cycling can occur daily.

My Mania

Mania is when the destruction occurs. Promiscuity, uncontrolled spending, grandiose behavior, are common. Often in the early stages there is boundless energy. People find me funny and magnetic. Employers are amazed at how hard and long I work. Then things start to change when there is talk about religion and UFO's and I stop eating and drink only caffeine to keep the high going. I may start to rhyme my words, a symptom known as "clanging". People around me will start to ask if I am "OK" I will become irritated at their questions because I know at this point that I am superhuman. My activity will increase and sleep will become unimportant. I will either dye or cut my own hair and start to draw on or redesign my clothing. I will pick up objects on the street and attach great spiritual significance and magical importance to these objects. I will even make some of them into jewelry and wear them as protective talismans. I will lose my job. My friends will become concerned for my safety and my health as my weight plummets to 160lbs (I usually weigh 200Lbs) Strangers will fear my energy and insane behavior. At this point I will become paranoid and delusional. I usually begin reading the bible because I am receiving direct messages from Jesus himself telling me that he will be arriving soon by spaceship. I am drawn to a particular place where I wait night after night for the arrival of the ship. When it doesn't arrive I begin to come down. It is usually at this point that I realize that I am having another "Breakdown".

My Depression

Depression can be mild and present itself as simple sadness. When it becomes problematic it usually starts to happen suddenly and I dip fast into a deep state of dark and paralyzing emptiness. This is characterized by a complete lack of physical energy and an inability to get out of bed. The simplest tasks such as shaving, getting dressed or brushing my teeth become impossible. Feelings of hopelessness and despair are common. Initially sugar consumption increases as well as other comfort foods in an attempt to change the mood. Energy levels drop and sleep becomes an escape from the painful daily grind. I once slept for three days in a row, only getting up to urinate and drink water. Suicidal thoughts begin to permeate my thinking and it is at this point that medication or hospitalization becomes necessary. Thankfully I have learned to spot the early signs and tell my doctor so that he can adjust my medicines accordingly.

My Mixed Mania

On occasion I will experience all of the aforementioned symptoms in a short period of time. It becomes confusing because I literally do not know whether I am coming or going. When mania and depression are experienced at the same time it is known as a "mixed state" I prefer the term "emotional rollercoaster" myself. Laughing one minute, crying the next, then feeling perfectly fine. This can be the hardest thing for a doctor to prescribe for, not to mention a stressful time for family, friends and patient. It is during these periods that I am most often asked if I suffer from multiple personality disorder.

My Rapid Cycling

My cycles occur all year long. The most obvious ones are in the spring when I become manic, and the winter when I become depressed. The high summer months bring the potential for extreme mania with psychosis. I cycle through all of these phases in varying degrees between the seasons. Occasionally I will go through a phase when I cycle through all of the mood states in a week. Things are better now. There are new medicines to help balance out the rough spots and my doctor and I are making real progress in choosing a plan of action that is working to balance me out all year!

December 10, 1998, 5 A.M. Halfway to Christmas. As I pad about my small but quaint Cape Cod apartment, I am amazed by the beginning of this writing, although, I guess, not too surprised, seeing as I bought this notebook weeks ago.

"You should write a book."

These words echo in my head like a tortuous mantra, well aware of my many failed attempts to commit my life story to paper. I wonder if this will be another half-filled notebook, tossed aside at the crest of another mood swing. Maybe. Maybe not.

The coffee is taking effect, and the voices in my head have increased to a murmur.

"You should really write a book."

"What a fascinating story."

"You've had a charmed life."

And, of course, the edgier voice, still shrill and clear, even after twenty years of therapy, the voice of a now-deceased stepparent that taunts from the grave:

"You've been on a permanent vacation your whole life."

It's no wonder to me that there are so many false starts to this story. Shame and dread hold hands and dare me to reveal the truth about myself. God, himself, sits at the throne of judgment, ready to cast me into the fiery pit, daring me to reveal my life, let alone publish it. This is familiar territory, so I sip some more coffee and plug away, my hand beginning to cramp, and I'm only on the second page. If only I had a word processor.

"Why don't you talk the book into a tape recorder and then have someone type it for you?"

This is a familiar voice, a caring, gentle voice. My response is that only a miracle will ever produce this book. There are too many demons. Even after years of therapy, medications and recovery, they stand firmly in front of me and dare me to move forward. Lighting another cigarette, inhaling deeply, I consider stopping, smoking not writing. My hand is cramping, my mind spinning, when suddenly a new voice, quiet, serene, and yet, possessing a distinct power, speaks plainly.

"Did it ever occur to you that the reason this is so hard, that your mind keeps throwing up blocks, is because the story you have to tell is so powerful that you will create quite a disturbance, if you tell it?" Yes. It has occurred to me. I am well aware of the fear. And I have experienced the judgment firsthand. The anger. The looks. The pointing. The whispers. Why on earth would I want to subject myself to that?

The answer comes clearly and quickly, but not before I have a chance to form a rebuttal, the by-product of habitual defensiveness.

"The truth will set you free," the still voice coaxes.

"What will my father think?" I respond meekly, returning to God's throne room.

Silence. Stillness. The refrigerator stops humming, and the only sound I hear is the clock ticking on the bookshelf next to my chair.

"Time heals everything."

An encouraging thought. I waited, wondering how to begin the story of my life.

"Start at the beginning."

Okay. Here goes.

I didn't have a normal childhood. There, I said it. What is normal? I suppose that, like many in my generation, the Brady Bunch or the Partridge family would be the standard. Actually, the Brady Bunch came close. At one point, my father, Bob, married

Debbie, my stepmother, and she and her children moved in with us; and that's where the resemblance to our TV counterparts began and ended. Oh, sure, we tried to be the perfect family, but the odds were stacked against us. There would be no neat, one-hour problem solving in our house. This was due to the fact that the players were not Marcia, Greg, Peter, et al. We were damaged goods and, no matter how heroic our efforts, our problems would soon engulf the house, smothering just about everything in sight. I know this sounds dramatic, and believe me, it is. I guess I should go back a little and explain. You see, before my dad remarried, we lived with our real mom, Judy. Judy, Judy, Judy, Judy. Dad was her second husband. There were three in all. I remember her as any child would remember their mother. She was beautiful, fun-loving, energetic, and yes, very dramatic. I would find out as an adult that she was also an alcoholic, a mental patient.Characteristics I would soon exhibit with a vengeance. Of course, as a child, I did not understand any of this. She was just Mom. What I did understand was that she was not like any of the moms in the neighborhood, or the moms on TV (which I was already addicted to watching). No, Judy was a firestorm. Big entrances, huge exits and lots of devastation in between. My dad was one of her many early casualties. I was then five years old but can still remember her words in the car as we drove down Elm Street in New Canaan, Connecticut.

"Where's Daddy?" I remember asking innocently.

"You have a new father. He will be at the house when we get home. His name is Loren Ludwig. You can call him Lud."

At the time, it seemed to me that Mom had taken Dad into a store and exchanged him for someone else. I guess this makes sense to a child of five. She said it so matter-of-factly that I don't really remember having any emotional response at the time.

"Will we see our old dad again?"

"Yes, dear. He'll pick you up on weekends."

I remember thinking, two dads. Neat-o. I was blissfully unaware that my life was about to be turned upside down and inside out, leaving me with emotional, physical and mental scars that would take a lifetime to heal.

I'm the youngest of four children: two older brothers and an older sister. I'm sure that my siblings have their own versions of the events that befell us in our childhood years; however, I can only tell you the story as I remember it. It's hard for me to tell for a few reasons. The first would be credibility. You see, I started to lie at a very early age. First to the neighbors, soon to everyone. So, of course, the voices in my head start to say, "You might as well give up this book idea for now, for if it were ever published, so many people would step forward to discredit you that it would be a complete waste of time."

But, I write anyway, critics be damned. Let 'em dig up the dirt. The truth will be out in the end.

I was six years old when the violence started. It infected our house like a cold virus and spread into the extended family, its source unknown, but a few key players were easily identified. The first, my middle brother, who seemed to have been born angry, and I suppose as the kid who shared his room and bunk bed, it was only natural that I would be the target of his not-so-pent-up aggression. Five years my senior, and much stronger, he landed punch after punch to my face and body. My most vivid memories consist of broken teeth, blood, and me running and screaming for Mom. She was my protector. I knew that I could count on her to deliver justice in the form of a beating with her hairbrush. Violence truly begets violence. Next, my stepfather: three hundred pounds, six feet four inches tall, a raging alcoholic. I look back with conflicting emotions of love and fear.

"Pull down your pants!"

His voice boomed, then the thick belt hit my bare behind and thighs.

Then there was the violence I witnessed. Frustrations bubbling over that no amount of alcohol seemed to quell. Mom hitting brothers, brothers hitting sister, stepfather hitting everyone, then the heavy silence, muffled crying. Nightmare-filled sleeps. Eight shows a week, matinee Sunday. The escape route was beginning to develop as I sank into myself, too small to fight, too scared to sit still. It was during this time that I began to lie and get caught. I did not seem to understand that the truth would have been easier on me. The beating I tried so hard to avoid in lying only became more severe and prolonged with each uncovered deceit.

"Why do you lie to me?" Mom would ask.

"I don't know."

And I didn't. Not then. I look back on those times and realize that it was a way to cope. I created my own reality in my head and presented it as truth. There was no guilt or shame, except when I got caught. All this did was help me to become a more proficient liar. A quick study, someone once said. A quick study but a very poor student. It was in school that I began to develop what seemed like the next step for a budding pathological liar. I became the class clown. In hindsight, I can see that I was a walking cry for help. However, at the time I needed attention, and I was beginning to see how humor could diffuse the most tense situations, with the home front battleground as my laboratory, TV sitcoms as my tutor, and sugar-coated cereals my fuel. I was quickly resented by my schoolmates, and I stole the teacher's focus away, ever the needy child. It's hard to look back without analyzing it because I've spent most of my adult life in one therapy or another. Then, of course, I had no idea what was going on. I only knew that I made 'em laugh, and that was my most powerful weapon. And I found out early on that I could sing! On key! My mother used to tell a story about how my kindergarten teacher had asked how long I had been taking singing lessons.

"He's only five years old," she would say with feigned exasperation, secretly full of pride. I had a natural gift.

My dad would say, "He gets that from me."

All I knew was that I was imitating the adults and it worked. They won't hurt you if you make 'em laugh. Sing a song.

"He's such a talented, happy child," the teachers would say. "If only he could stay focused."

"He has trouble paying attention in class and tends to disrupt group activities," one teacher would write in a first-grade report card. Laughing and singing. Hide the pain.

"How'd you cut your eye, Scott?" a teacher would ask.

"I fell."

Small lie, make eye contact, smile, no blinking.

"Looks like it hurts."

"Nah!"

Smile. Stuff the feelings. Erase the memory. Keep 'em laughing. Throw 'em off the scent.

"You're a special child," the principal would say.

Different. Strange. Soon school would become as unsafe as home, and my flight from reality would take on a new dimension.

It was Christmas Eve, 1968. We piled into the family station wagon to head off to Gringa and Nana's house. My mother's parents lived in a tonier part of town, although at age seven I don't think I yet understood that money could have produced the effect of magic in the way I perceived my grandparents' house. To me, then, their beautiful home was merely an extension of them as Grama and Granpa. I was oblivious to the hard work and struggle that went into making their surroundings so opulent compared to the stark contrast in my mother's house. And Christmas Eve was a time when things shone brighter than any other time at the house on Woodridge Circle. The drive seemed to take forever in those days, though as an adult I can make it in ten minutes.

On this particular evening, my mother announced in her matter-of-fact way, as we pulled onto the circle that led to their driveway, that Nana would "not be here tonight."

"Where is she?" someone asked in a small voice.

"She's gone to heaven."

Case closed.

What I remember next is my grandfather, glass of amber liquid in hand, tears streaming down his face, while his descendants gathered up the loot from under the large tree.

"Why are you crying, Gringa?" I asked.

He looked perplexed, stunned and sad. Then he threw his glass against the wall in rage. The next thing I knew we were all in the car again, heading home with piles of presents and visions of Santa Claus looking suspiciously like a certain aunt of ours. Wondering where Nana was. And if heaven were such a great place, as Mom convinced me it was, what was Gringa so angry about and why was everyone always whispering? So, I prayed to God, as naively as any child prays, asking him to take care of Nana. I also wondered what suicide meant, too afraid to ask.

Christmas came and went, and New Year's Eve arrived, and a bond developed with my sister, Ann. It was on that night when I first discovered what it was like to laugh uncontrollably. Mom and Lud were out on the town, and I was left in my sister's care. I realize that even if I were to tell the whole story of how my big sister made me laugh till I peed in my pants, that only I would find the story very funny. You know—it was one of those "you had to be there" kind of things. It involved one of those long, drawn-out jokes with an eventual punch line that was so stupid only an eight-year-old would laugh, but I could tell by the gleam in her eye, she knew that she had me. It was a lame story about a stolen turkey sandwich and its eventual discovery. I don't think I've ever laughed as hard as I did that night. It was such an exciting evening, and we got to stay up and watch the ball come down in Times Square. Staying up until midnight, just like the grownups. It would be a few years until I found out what grownups did on New Year's Eve.

The next few years are a blur, except for the escalation of the war between my m other and stepfather. Their fights became louder and more violent, and the police began to appear from time to time. The day after always included a debriefing, the chief subject:

Don't tell the neighbors, teachers or anyone outside of the house what happened here last night. And especially, don't tell your father.

He would come and rescue us on weekends, adding to our escape with the latest Walt Disney film. My dad—funny, smart, handsome, gentle—is the opposite of my stepfather. My sister and I would spend years trying to re-unite him with our mom, to no avail. He never laid a hand on us, and in the eyes of a child, he was heroic, his faults overlooked in the shadow of our stepfather's heavy hand.

By age nine, it was becoming apparent to me that I was not like the other boys around me. I was much more interested in playing with the girls than with the boys. I played house at lunchtime, and the boys began to tease me with words I wouldn't understand until much later in life. This only heightened my fears of my own gender, which I viewed with dread. All boys ever did was taunt me, hit me, kick me, tease me, and humiliate me. The girls would hide and protect me, save me from the dreaded men. While other boys played football and cars, I played cheerleader and Barbie, much more at home in the softer, gentler world of pom-poms and Dreamhouses. My mother indulged me, even getting me an easy-bake oven. I cooked foul-tasting cakes with a one-hundred-watt light bulb and fed them happily to the family dog. It was at this time when the men in the house started trying to butch me up and the breaking point that would shatter my world into pieces that I'm still picking up thirty years later.

Here are the events that occurred as near as I can remember them. Shortly after Nana committed suicide, Gringa remarried an exceptional woman named Dorothy. She was everything Nana wasn't: outgoing, vibrant, funny, and demonstrative. I believe that God places angels in people's lives for a reason, and Grandma Dee was the angel my family needed more than ever. She and Mom became fast friends, though it would be considerably longer for the rest of the family to warm up to her. I adored her. She was a tall woman with brilliant, white hair like Gringa's and they looked smashing together. That summer, she took us to her beach house and club at Shippan Point and introduced us to New York City. She was generous and loving, and had an infectious spirit that touched everyone

she came into contact with. I suppose a lot of people were
intimidated by her, but I didn't realize that then. I took refuge
in her size and strength.

   It was in March of 1971 that her strength, all of our strengths,
would be put to the test. She and Gringa loaded us all up in their
Lincoln Continental and took us into the city. We were going to meet
up with my mother and stepfather and see them off on a reconciliation
cruise, my stepfather's last-ditch attempt to save his marriage.
   A few weeks before, he and Mom had had one of their most
violent fights. My stepfather had locked us all out. Apparently,
my mother tried to stab him, and all I clearly remember is his big
hand, reaching out and pushing her backward down our front
stairs onto the cement walkway. She scraped her face on the
pavement and came up bloody and mad. She sent us to a neighbor's
house to call the police, and they were there when we returned. I
accompanied my mom, with my brother, to the hospital, and when
they asked me who my father was, I remember my mother laughing
as I announced, "I don't have one!"
   Lud showed up the next week with tickets for a cruise and I
remember crying the night before and begging Mom not to go.
   I kept saying, "You're not going to come back!" over and over.
   She reassured me that she was, but my gut told me differently.

   We all arrived at the shipping piers on Manhattan's West Side
and boarded to say goodbye to Lud and Mom. I remember hiding
in the closet of their cabin and everyone searching for me. As the
call was sounded for all non-passengers to leave the ship, I
remembered my protest from the previous night, convinced that
something bad was going to happen. I was escorted off by my
grandparents and we were taken to Radio City Music Hall to see a
show. The movie was *The Out-of-Towners* with Sandy Dennis and
Jack Lemmon. My sister and I imitated Sandy Dennis all the way
back to New Canaan, saying, "Oh, my God!" And the humor,

coupled with Grandma Dee's reassurance that all would be well and I would see Mom in a week, greatly improved my mood.

I went back to school that Monday, missing Mom terribly. Time seemed to stand still as I anticipated her return. On Wednesday, I came over the hill from the bus stop and was surprised to see a crowd of cars and people in front of our house. I recognized one of the cars as my Uncle Howard's and Aunt Jan's, and I started to run, carrying my new violin with me. The next memory I have is of sitting in the living room and my aunt saying she had something important to tell us. I asked if I could tune my new violin, eager to impress everyone, and she said sure.

"Your mother has had an accident."

"Is she okay?" I asked.

"No, sweetheart. I'm afraid she isn't coming home. She's dead."

Time stood completely still for the first time in my life. I sat there, stunned, with my violin on my lap. The next period of time was an absolute blur. Numbness, tears, and still more numbness, followed by rage at God. First Nana, now Mom. It was not fair. I want Mom back!

We spent the week at Gringa's and I remember Grandma Dee making me waffles. I also remember the kids at school whispering. It would be years later before I even knew how shattered I was, and even twenty-eight years later, as I write these words, the pain is restored, though dulled and dissipated through years of therapy and the sweet passage of time. Time heals everything.

The next few years were a numbing blur. My siblings and I were shipped off to different relatives to live, separated by towns and distance, while my birth father fought for custody. Ann went to my Aunt Joanne's and Uncle Al's, Stephen was in a private school, Jeffrey took off with his rock band, and I went to live in Guilford, Connecticut, with my mother's brother and his wife, as well as their five dogs and two cats. My dad would visit on weekends but always returned me to my aunt and uncle on Sunday evenings. I would plead with him to not take me back to the strange house, in the strange town, but the courts had tied his hands, and he was doing his best to get custody. I felt abandoned once again, and began to retreat further into fantasy, creating my own world where nothing and no one could touch me.

One of the stipulations for Dad to regain custody was that he must remarry. He did, and we were reunited as a family with a new mother. I was very happy to be back with my sister, but now I had two stepsisters and a stepbrother to deal with, as well as a new mom, Debbie. She was beautiful and bubbly, and I liked her instantly. I couldn't have known the rocky road that lay ahead, for I was just so happy to be back with my family. She worked very hard to make us a nice home, but she couldn't have been prepared to handle four children, all of whom were experiencing the loss of their mother and beginning to exhibit symptoms of that loss, as well as the damage of being raised in a violent alcoholic environment. We became a handful rather quickly and, within a few short days, the battle lines were drawn.

Puberty, alcohol, drugs and the discovery that I was homosexual, coupled with mental illness, grief, and no self-esteem, would make me one of the larger, unsolvable problems in the household. My stepmother became increasingly bitter and hostile as I began to lie, cheat, and steal in an attempt to cover up my addictions and gay life. And, in my denial, I thought she had the problem! Eventually, I would leave home and not return for many years.

I went to my first gay bar at the age of sixteen. I was appearing in a production of *Jesus Christ Superstar* in Darien, Connecticut, and the director asked me if I would like to go to New York and see a Broadway show and spend the weekend. It was the weekend that would establish a pattern in my life for many years to come.

We took the train to Grand Central and walked across Fifth Avenue to Times Square. I'd been to New York many times, but its size and energy had never impressed me the way it did that weekend. It was my first Broadway show, *Eubie,* and I remember very little of it because my hormones were raging and I was about to discover a world full of men just like me!

After the show, we walked, my date (whose name I cannot remember) and I, to Charlie's Restaurant on Forty-fifth Street between Broadway and Eighth Avenue, and as we entered the room, I experienced something I had not been aware of before. Men, mostly waiters, were paying attention to me. Physically. First, the two hosts, who seem overly friendly, as if I were a long-lost friend. I don't think I realized that I was so obviously gay and then, one by one, the waiters came by and gave me their phone numbers. I had never been as popular in my life and I shone in the attention, much to my "date's" despair. By the end of the dinner, I had five phone numbers, and I gently inquired if it would be all right to go exploring. He was disappointed, but said, "Sure, go ahead," and I began my promiscuous life, though I would have no idea what the word meant until years later.

I called the first host. From his house I called the first waiter, second, third, fourth, then the second host, who took me to the Spike and then the Mineshaft, where I spent the remainder of the weekend drinking, smoking pot and having sex before returning to Connecticut without ever reconnecting with my "date." I dropped out of the production and began a secret life of NYC on the weekends, telling my parents that I was sleeping over at a friend's house. I discovered cocaine, LSD, poppers, Quaaludes, and any other drug you could provide, and began using them daily. I paid for them with my body and stealing, and this created a fair amount of Christian guilt; I was so mad at God and the raw deal I felt life had given me. Alcohol and drugs provided the anesthetic and deceit the social lubricant, as I drifted farther out of reality, making up a different story for each new person while reveling in my newly found hedonism, and all the while pretending to be straight to my girlfriend, family, friends, and classmates. Lying about where I'd been and with whom soon became a daily event, as well as covering up my drug and alcohol use. It became impossible to keep track of all of the lies, and I began to get caught.

My grades suffered, and I spent my junior year in summer school making up classes I'd skipped to get high.

My senior year and the next five or six years after are a blur of events and emotional breakdowns. I remember many incidences, primarily for the drama, but the chronology is a mystery, even after many years of sobriety. I was still making my weekend excursions to New York City and my awareness of gay life had expanded beyond the bars to nightclubs and after-hour places.

I was still seeing two of the waiters and one host from Charlie's, and one Friday night David, the host, suggested I check out Studio 54. I'd heard about the infamous disco, and now I found myself standing in front of it, in a borrowed shirt, trying to get the doorman's attention, hoping to get picked, but not expecting it, thinking of grade school and being the last one picked for kickball, due to my lack of physical grace and feminine tendencies. What I was unaware of at the time is that being young, gay, and cute would open almost any door in the late seventies, and I reacted like a stunned beauty contestant when the doorman singled me out for entry. Me. You mean me. I entered through the door, into the velvet hallway, and checked my coat.

Tuesday, December 15, 1998, 5 P.M. I'm up again at the crack of dawn, and for the first time in my life writing is becoming an obsession. Something I *must* do. Questioning my motivation reveals a number of possible truths. Bestseller becomes a mantra, and my frustration and apprehension build up, for who am I trying to presume that my life story merits that kind of attention?

It's the kind of thinking that frequently sabotages any creative effort, carrying me away on imaginary excursions of success while polluting the creative process, and tangling thoughts by turning the flashlight of judgment on every word that is thought of, most likely a key source of writer's block. Bestseller, bestseller. This is a common problem for me. Cart before the horse. Writing acceptance speeches in my head before even thinking about auditioning for anything that would bring me close to a nomination for the coveted award. Writing a story of scandalous gossip, celebrity encounters that the reading public so hungers for, in a transparent attempt to fill my bank account, or do I tell the story of survival, first of a horrific childhood, then an epidemic that has devastated so many, yet left me with the luxury of bearing witness? My inner critic wakes up, fueled by a second cup of coffee, and announces his presence with a familiar barrage of anti-Scott notices:

"Who are you to write a memoir? You're nobody. Why would anyone want to read about an alcoholic, drug-addicted fag with AIDS, from a broken home, with no formal education or writing experience? You're just looking for a quick buck, so you can get on with your self-satisfied existence, you sick fuck!"

Enough already! I shout inside my head, loud enough to stop the demonic voice, but certain that it hasn't been exorcised.

I'm writing this for me, Mr. Critic. It's therapy. If no one buys it, if I never get it published, so what? At least it has been written, and all the shit in my head has been put down on paper, so thank you for sharing and fuck you very much.

Now, where was I? Oh, yeah . . . Studio 54.

"Why did God create gay men?"

"So fat girls would have someone to dance with."

This would be the voice of my inner comic, showing up no doubt to try and take the sting out of the critic's attack. Make 'em laugh. No matter how old and cheesy the joke.

Suddenly, a fight erupts between my ears.

"No one wants to hear about Studio 54. It's been done."

But I spent the night with Robin Williams and his wife and manager at the Essex House . . .

"Yeah, right. I'm sure they still talk about it. You remember that busboy my manager fucked that night."

I met Cheryl Tiegs. Andy Warhol. I got fired for sleeping with Steve Ruebell's boyfriend.

"Big whoop! You were just a busboy, and for eight weeks. They saw the movie, all three of them. Move on. Get a life. Give up this writing nonsense and get a job, for Chrissakes!"

I can't get a job. I'm sick.

"Funny, you don't look sick. Are you sure this isn't another one of your scams?"

Fuck you! Eat me! Blow me!

"Shut up!"

Silence. God. No wonder you never finish anything.

High school ended with a whimper and I left for New York City an hour after graduation ceremonies ended. My diploma was blank, withheld because of skipped gym classes and incomplete English assignments. No matter. I would soon be a famous actor, singer, model, dancer, waiter, busboy, failure, coke whore.

I arrived at Stephen's Upper West Side apartment with my carload of possessions and a perplexed expression of "Aren't you happy to see me?"

"You can't stay here. I have a roommate."

Oh, well, I'll think of something. Let's see. First stop, Grand Central Station. Deposit clothes in a locker, then on to the St. Marks Baths, the Saint, Studio, Crisco Disco, Mineshaft, Spike, party 'til you drop. The world is your oyster.

Unless you are a drug-addicted, homeless, jobless, penniless high school dropout.

I spent the next year bed-hopping, stealing, drinking, drugging, and wandering the streets of the Big Apple as the wind left my sails, slowly but surely.

I was becoming *persona non grata* at the bars and clubs, my reputation preceding me, my damaged brain deteriorating.

Wandering through Times Square, tripping on LSD, I decided

that there was only one way out. I joined the navy.

If you've ever been to Times Square, you may have noticed a glass booth with Army, Air Force, Navy, Marines printed on the side. The U.S. government is very smart in having this location, for Times Square is a magnet for lost boys like me, ripe for the picking. A few good men.

I entered the little glass-enclosed booth and was greeted by a smiling Chief Petty Officer named Stewart.

"I want to join the navy," I said matter-of-factly, through a kaleidoscope of colors and trails, putting my butchest foot forward, wondering if my dilated pupils would disqualify me. Make 'em laugh. Not now, comic. This is serious.

"Why do you want to be in the navy, son?"

I guess they are required to ask this.

"I feel like my life has no direction. I'm wandering the streets, and I think it would make my dad proud. He was in the navy."

This seems to satisfy Petty Officer Stewart, and before long, I'm on a plane to Great Lakes, Illinois.

If you've ever seen the movie *Private Benjamen*, you just might be able to imagine a slightly gayer version, starring me.

Great Lakes Naval Training Center. What have I gotten myself into this time, I think as I watch my shoulder-length hair fall around me, the sadistic barber smiling at my disapproving look.

I volunteered for triple-threat Company 903—the band, chorus and drill team—thinking this will somehow give me an easier ride. What it does instead is add two extra weeks of boot camp and tosses me into McHale's Navy with a bunch of other lazy closet cases.

I learn to polish shoes, make a bed, swab a deck, buff a deck, wait in line, and sing a stirring rendition of *Anchors Away*. Early to rise, early to bed, and oh, the naked men in the shower! Six weeks, seven weeks, and I start to come unglued, unfamiliar with the concept of detoxing and increasingly aware of the feelings stirring in my heart and groin. Fear of discovery takes on new meaning in a time when "don't ask, don't tell" means "make one false move, faggot, and you're dead."

I do my best to conceal my desires, but without the benefit of alcohol and drugs, my acting ability is severely stunted.

And the voices in my head are about to become audible to everyone as I experience the first of three very public nervous breakdowns, or as the naval psychiatrist labels in his discharge report, "Transient Mental Disorder." Those words still amaze me. He's crazy, but it's just a passing, temporary thing.

I'm not exactly sure what precipitated the next events, but I can guess that the angel-dusted joint I smoked while AWOL had something to do with it. It's very clear how it ended. It was about 9 P.M., I was in my room at hospital corps school, watching TV, when the voices in my head instructed me to follow them. Unfortunately, they neglected to mention that something other than my underwear and one sock might be appropriate attire for the trip. Down the hall, into the co-ed lounge, the pathway parted as stunned recruits got out of the way of the wild-eyed, half-naked lunatic. Out of the door and into the snow, I headed toward the naval hospital across the small bridge. My pace quickened, aware that ground watches were in hot pursuit. The security watch at the front desk did not notice me, which of course, in my altered state, caused me to believe that invisibility was a newfound power. I slipped past him and up the stairwell to the fifth floor, which, unbeknownst to me at the time, housed the psychiatric unit I would call home for the next month.

I would soon discover the presence of God. Sadly, we wouldn't be on speaking terms for two more rounds.

Sometimes, I think God has a sick sense of humor. Why else would he or she consistently reveal him or herself to a known pathological liar who hears voices and has a history of mental illness?

My theory is that this is part of life's built-in security systems. God's secrets are safe when witnessed by the boy who cried "Wolf!"

Honorable discharge under medical conditions.
I read this over and over, and keep wondering if it's a misprint.

Back to NYC, falling into familiar patterns of bars, baths, and hustling, I would soon meet God face to face, in the form of hundreds of everyday people just like you.

The train to New Canaan takes about an hour and fifteen minutes from Grand Central. I arrive at my sister's garage apartment and revel in the retelling of my latest adventure, totally unaware that an even greater meltdown is about to occur.

I *do* remember how this one began. I went to a bar in New Canaan called Brock's, wearing my navy uniform, thinking it would gain me respect, with no intention of revealing my discharged status . . .

The bar is filled, mostly by college kids who were home for the holidays, friends and drug-buddies who have managed to move on to higher learning.

"Hey, it's Jerk-off Jordan!" someone yells as I enter the bar area, and I recognize my fellow high school pot-heads. I laugh good-naturedly, knowing full well that the joke is on me, oiling my way over, hoping to score a high. I can't remember any of the names of faces, but I vividly recall the package of white powder that is dumped into a draft beer and passed to me. I smile and chug the whole thing, looking up at five stunned faces, wiping foam off my chin as the realization of what just happened hits me.

"You asshole! That was for everyone!" MDA for six, and yes, I drank the whole thing! My sister talked me down from the trip, and I left town for the next two years. New York City streets again. Lost, alone, hungry, and frightened. Nowhere to go. Nothing to do.

This time I joined the Moonies.

It's been said that God watches out for drunks and fools. I'm convinced that I survived the next three years of my life simply because I fall into *both* categories.

It was about 10:10 A,M, same day: I've just returned home after taking a break from this writing in an attempt to walk off the three cups of coffee I have consumed in the past hour, only to proceed to walk to a local coffee shop, the only one open in our little seasonal seaside resort community in the dead of winter, where I consume two more cups. Coffee has become my drug of choice for the nineties, a legal choice, though not necessarily a good one for someone prone to mania and hearing voices. So, here I sit, pen in hand, wondering how to proceed with a story that seems to so desperately want to be told, wanting to hurry up the story out of fear that I might be boring the readers by now with my endless tales of woeful, drug-induced, psychotic episodes.

"Why don't you just skip the next section and write about your recovery?" a slightly pained and caffeinated voice coaxes.

The sun streams in my living room window. The furnace starts up and a warm wind blows past my head from the vent next to the couch where I sit, pen in hand, staring blankly, wired to the gills on coffee, unsure of which direction to take.

Get to the good part. My own calm thought, not the voices in my head.

I think about what the "good" part of the story is.

"You know, the part where you find God, and start to get well."

Is this a thought or a voice, I wonder. Maybe just a normal person talking to himself.

Write about rehab, group therapy, your spiritual awakening, your healing of your past, your HIV medication, and how good you feel. Your survival. Be upbeat. You've said enough about the past. Talk about the present and how you came to this beautiful place. How you learned to quiet your mind, amend your mistakes, find peace and serenity. Write about your survival and gratitude to the doctors, therapists, friends, lovers who have helped you. I recognize the voice. My inner cheerleader, growing ever more urgent, desperately coaxing me away from memories, circumstances and old wounds, protecting me from myself.

It would be a relief to write about this stuff, I think for now, as I check my emotions; I wish there was a way to finish this story in a hurry. The anxiety stems from the fact that I know I must tell the whole thing. I take a deep breath and try to relax, knowing that no amount of caffeine will get me through the next part any faster. I guess I just pick up where I left off and try to ignore my renewed fear that I will never finish this project. That I will get bogged down in the emotional repercussions of disclosure and this notebook will share the fate of many past attempts.

Suddenly, I realize that I've gotten farther along than ever before. Maybe this time I'll actually finish, I think, waiting for the voices. Silence. Nothing. No critic, no comic. No self-defeating self-loathing. Calm.

I return to where I left off.

I met two women on the streets of New York. They were bright-eyed and smiling. I was cold, hungry, and desperate, though if you'd asked me, I would have replied:

"I'm fine, thank you." Stoic as ever.

"Would you like to come to dinner?" the blonde one said.

"Sure." I needed a meal. We walked up Fifth Avenue toward Forty-third Street, and they told me they were with an organization called CARP, College Association for the Research of Principles.

"I'm not in college."

It didn't matter. I was welcome to come to dinner. We entered a building that looked like a church and was filled with happy people, some of whom were laying out trays of food. All vegetarian. Not a burger in sight. Oh, well, I'm starving. After dinner, we all helped clean up, and then we were treated to a slide show of the CARP Center in Tarrytown, New York, and invited (more like pressured) to attend a weekend seminar. I was oblivious to what was really going on until we arrived in Tarrytown in the dead of night.

The following morning, we were awakened at the crack of dawn. They promised us breakfast, but first we were treated to calisthenics and a sing-along. After breakfast, we entered a tent where, for the first time since I joined up with the two nice girls who invited me to dinner, the name Reverend Sun Yung Moon was mentioned.

You could have knocked me over with a feather. I sat in stunned silence as they continued the lecture, which was followed by another strong-arm suggestion that we stay for a two-week study course.

"Take me back to the city right now," I demanded.

I was immediately surrounded by a small group of Moonie zealots who tried to convince me that it was Satan trying to get me to leave my newfound spiritual family. It might have worked, too, for they were harmless, good-hearted people and I must admit it, I enjoyed the sing-along. However, I was beginning to detox and happy hour wasn't on the menu.

They convinced me to spend the night and think it over. After numerous lectures, exercises, and sing-alongs, I and my fellow abductees were led to a barracks-like building for a rest. As soon as everyone was asleep, plus another hour just to be on the safe side, I made my escape. Sneaking out a side door, hiding behind trees, over a stone wall, behind a bush and then breaking into a run, I reached a main highway where I began hitchhiking. No one had followed me. I started to laugh, imagining how silly I must have looked when no one was actually chasing me, and then relief swept over me when I got a ride, taking me all the way back to Manhattan.

I had no money, no job, no home, and no prospects. So I decided to return to New Canaan. Knowing that I couldn't go to my father's house, I showed up on the doorstep of my childhood home. The same steps my mother had been pushed down, almost ten years earlier. I knocked on the door, and it was answered by a very surprised stepfather.

He was just as big as I remembered him to be. I asked if I

could come in. I told him I had nowhere to go and asked if I could live with him until I got myself together. I found a job at a cheese market and began drinking larger and larger amounts of alcohol. Things would have been great except it wasn't my alcohol to drink. It was my stepfather's and he needed it as much, if not more than me, by then. After a few serious arguments, and threats of violence, I had the first spiritual experience of consequence and began my descent out of the living hell that my life had become.

December 16, 7 A.M.

It occurs to me that I have been absorbed with the calamities of childhood for most of my adult life. Today, I will write about the things I never have written about. The things that kept me going through all the loss and sadness, pain and tears. After all, drugs and alcohol can only deaden the pain so much and, in my self-centeredness, it is easy to overlook both sides of the story. I would not be alive today if I had not been loved and cared for.

Between the beatings, death and loss, humiliation and shame, there was love and guidance, and plenty of it. It was dished out in enormous helpings, by many angels who recognized the need and filled the void, I believe, by God's grace.

Guidance counselors, aunts and uncles, teachers, family friends, all took turns trying to counsel, comfort and help, heal and protect, a family that was being ripped apart and, as the youngest, I received the lion's share of their attentions.

There were also good times. Laughter was in abundance and provided a refuge for everyone. Dad was the chief purveyor of humor, always ready with a joke or funny story to lift spirits. There were trips to zoos, museums, the beach and movies, dinner, parties. And music, lots of music, dancing and singing. For every new hurt and trauma, there were plenty of rescues.

"What are you writing about this for? No one wants to hear about good stuff. Stick to the horror and tragedy. It sells."

Thank you for sharing that, heard voice of doom. However, it's time to start balancing out the story for if it were all horror, I would not have survived to tell it. The voice subsides.

It's amazing how tight a grip gloom and doom has. But not today. This writing is about letting go of the past, forgiving, though not forgetting. It's a daunting task, and I wonder which side will prevail. After all, a lot of my family did not survive and those who did are battle-weary.

Still, there is much to hope for so I will return to telling my tale of woe for a moment, confident the angels are on the way.

There would be one more major drama before God's grace extended its hand in the form of a beautiful woman and the road to salvation would become visible.

My stepfather threw me out after hearing through the local grapevine that I thought he had pushed my mother off the boat. I was in the habit of talking big while drunk, and in a small town, news like that travels pretty fast.

I made a beeline for NYC, returning to a life of drugs, booze, sex and self-abuse, ending up in a cocaine dealer's house on Manhattan's Lower West Side. I was allowed to live there under the condition that I sell coke to help pay the rent, but pretty soon I began snorting the profits and found myself in the grip of a relentless cycle of very highs and extra lows.

Ever the creative problem solver, I decided that what I needed was a vacation. Somewhere warmer where I could soak up the sun and get off cocaine. I had no money but my roommate offered me a ticket and decided to join me. I said that I would come up with some cash to pay for a hotel and off we went to Montego Bay, Jamaica, in the dead of winter, 1983.

Unbeknownst to my traveling companion, I was unable to secure any cash for the trip, and when we arrived in Montego Bay, I discovered that the Doctor's Cave Beach Hotel would extend credit so we headed there where I began to sign for everything while scrambling to find a way to pay for it.

Cocaine was quickly replaced with rum punch, fueling my

delusion, as the hotel, drink and food bills skyrocketed.

I need to say here that it still engenders feelings of shame, years later, as I write this, a free man, when recalling this incident. I am not proud of my behavior, though there is some comfort in knowing that I was not in my right mind when this event occurred.

It was time to pay the bill. I had no money. My phone calls to the U.S. had yielded nothing for I had long ago burned the last bridge. The police were called. Rick suggested we make a run for the airport, but ever the demented optimist, I said,

"No, you go home. I may need your help, and there's no sense us both getting in trouble. I'll stay here and handle this."

I was still convinced that I could talk my way out of the situation. A quick study. Charming. A good boy, though slightly unfocused.

Rick left. I turned on the charm and assured the hotel manager that everything would be taken care of. He agreed with me and I found myself sitting in an eight-foot-by-ten-foot jail cell with nineteen other animals.

The 14 Barrett Street jail is located in a part of Jamaica that they do not show in any of the travel brochures which Rick and I poured over in our cocaine-and-alcohol-induced haze. It is located in a neighborhood that no tourist would visit by choice. Corrugated tin shacks make up most of its buildings, and its streets are narrow and dusty, overcrowded with Jamaica's poor and underprivileged.

The jail is probably the least glamorous of all its structures, resembling a baseball dugout with bars, or a concrete bomb shelter, half set in a dirt hill. I am led in handcuffs from the police car, wearing shorts, no shirt, my pierced nipple with gold ring visible for all to see. It dawns on me that I am not in a gay-friendly country, and my dread and fear increase as I realize that I am about to be locked up with the group of men in the third cell who were yelling "Ay, white man!" as I was being led to the cell door. The guard, a large, mean-looking woman, shoved me into the cell, which had a metal door with about a foot of bar space on top, and it took a few moments for my eyes to adjust to the cell's contents, having just been in the bright Jamaican sun a few minutes earlier, all the while repeating to myself, "This isn't happening" as if somehow this mantra would magically transport me back home, like Dorothy in *The Wizard of Oz*.

Reality intruded when my eyes began to focus and I began to hear voices outside of my head, in a familiar yet unfriendly chorus: "Blood clot, Bamba, Rast-clot," interspersed with "White man" and "Batte Boy," a word I knew meant "You're a dead man, faggot!"

My palms sweat and my heart races as I write this from the safety of my little Cape Cod home. Time relegated it as a movie that I played in long ago or a story to tell a sympathetic therapist or stunned crowd of party guests glibly rendered, with me as the tragic hero of international injustice, sort of a self-fancied, delusional gay Agent 007. The truth, as I recall it now, is that if I had consumed anything other than rum punch that week, I would have shit myself immediately. Reality continued to intrude as my life flashed before my eyes and I attempted to grasp how I ended up where I was.

This may be the one time in my life, however, when my manic-depressive, drug-addicted, delusional mind, coupled with my ability to think fast, stuff feelings and transform myself into someone else, saved my ass. Make 'em laugh. Sing a song. You're the victim here, I reassured myself.

The cell was a small rectangle with a bench on each side and against its rear wall. Every inch of bench was occupied with four more men sitting on the floor, and me facing them, my back against the metal door. To my right, a plastic bucket about half full, a stench of urine. The air was hot and still and the silence heavy with tension as the occupants assessed the new addition to their overcrowded cell. This strange, wild-eyed American tourist, half-naked, with a shiny gold ring penetrating his right nipple.

Oh, well, I thought. Try and break the ice.

"How's everyone doing?"

God. I sounded like Julie on *The Love Boat*.

Silence. Then: "Ay, white man! What are you in for?"

I launched into my tale of woe, doing my best macho imitation, turning Rick into my girlfriend, and the whole hotel thing into a domestic squabble, where she takes the money and runs.

Someone laughs. Others join in.

Keep going, I think. They're eating it up.

Introductions are made.

"I'm Quinte," a tall, handsome man with glistening skin and mischievous eyes says with a large grin.

I would spend the next twenty-seven days in this small room closer to death than ever before, as my brilliant cover-up slowly unraveled.

I had never been in jail before. Movies and television were my only reference, and I called my memory for reference and did my best to act and talk tough. My stepmother used to tell me that if I kept my behavior up, I would end up in jail and have to eat bread and water. I'd dismissed it then, but as my first jail meal was served, the memory flooded in, no longer amusing. It was bread. A large chunk of bread.

"This is it?" I said numbly.

Quinte said, "Except on Sundays, we get rice, with goat meat."

The bucket in the corner was our toilet as I'd suspected. I'm not sure if it's possible to not take a dump for four weeks, but I do not recall ever having taken one the whole time I was incarcerated. I also lost twenty-seven pounds, one for each day of jail time. The bread and water diet. I don't recommend it.

By now, Rick had arrived in New York, and I used my one phone call (just like the movies) to call him. I remember saying, "Please, call my father."

This is worse than *Midnight Express.*

The chronology of my total experience is blurry, but I will share some of the highlights, which are permanently emblazoned on my memory.

I went to court five times in four weeks. We were led out of our cells, handcuffed, then chained together. Led out of our dugout to a flatbed truck with wooden rails, driven through the streets to the courthouse past local citizens who booed and hissed, some throwing rotten fruit.

At the courthouse, we were led into a large holding cell, before being brought before the judge. Four times the clerk read the charges: "Trying to obtain credit by fraud."

Four times I replied: "Not guilty."

Only to be returned quickly to the holding cell, then back to the cement holding cell. I waited patiently for news from Rick, as my faith dwindled. I was informed that I would be tried, and if found guilty, sent to prison for not days, but years.

The final week in jail began with a man in the cell next to ours being beaten to death during a fight and my audience becoming increasingly suspicious and hostile to the white man who made "jail talk," promising to send money, food, and cigarettes "as soon as my family gets me out of this place."

I did not sleep much that last week. Each day, someone new would challenge my stories about my girlfriend, my pierced nipple, and the family who had not freed me. On the day of my release, Quinte, my former friend, said,

"Jordan, if you come back from court today, you are a dead man."

I knew he wasn't kidding, and I began to pray like never before.

I arrived at the courthouse to find a lawyer had been hired from a family friend to assist in my release. The hotel bill was paid as well as a fine, and I was escorted to the airport and put on a plane to New York, in a state of shock. As I entered the plane, I noticed the people were all staring at me. I couldn't figure out why. I was just so relieved to be free and heading home. It did not occur to me that I had not bathed for weeks, and the wrinkled clothing I had on smelled from being rolled up in my duffel bag, hanging loosely off my now-skinny frame.

"What on earth happened to you?" a friendly Jamaican stewardess asked.

Still delusional, I pour my story out, still accepting no responsibility, believing I was a victim of bad luck; I had a captive audience and soon my fellow passengers were consoling me and comforting me.

I had my first drink on the plane. We all sang "God Bless America," as the plane landed. Another brilliant snow job. Thought I believed my own lies by now, convinced that my ever-changing version of the truth was real. Naturally, I was mystified that when I passed through customs to be greeted by my father, the family friend who orchestrated my release and his gorgeous wife, they were not elated to see me. I know now what really happened.

They listened to my story in the car on the way back to New Canaan. Intoxicated by my freedom, I babbled on for the whole ride. When we reached the town line, my father spoke.

"You can't stay with us. Debbie doesn't want you in the house."

Silence. I had no idea what to say.

"We arranged for you to stay with some friends of ours," the nice woman in the seat next to me said, smiling.

I had no way of knowing she would be the angel sent to point me out of hell towards a life that even in my wildest dreams I could never have imagined.

She came to see me the next day. We went to lunch and then to Mead Park to feed the ducks and she listened intently as I told my life-long tale of woe. I didn't know it then, but she was well versed in helping people like me get help.

I believe in angels. Not the white-winged, cloud hoppers of Christian folklore, but the hand and heart of God, personified in human form. Men and women who give their time and energy to help lost, suffering souls like me find their way home.

In 1984, I entered into my first alcoholism treatment center in Norwalk Hospital (the same hospital where I was born twenty-three years earlier), addicted to cocaine, marijuana, alcohol, cigarettes, caffeine, sex, and any person, place, or thing that took me away from my pent-up shame, pain and rage.

I still thought that my childhood that was the problem, for it had been a convenient excuse that had become habit. I was the only gay person on the unit, and I had just been diagnosed with what was then called ARC or AIDS-related complex.

The next bit of writing may prove extremely difficult for I am, and have always been, a person who has needed approval from as many people as possible; I fear that you, the reader, if not disgusted by me after the Jamaica incident, will surely dislike me when you see how I use my sickness and childhood to manipulate the angels of my early recovery attempts. My own self-hatred has resurfaced and I am glad to have a therapy appointment to discuss this so that I may proceed with my story, for it is cathartic, however painful, to face the truth of who I was, knowing that I would soon become who I believe my creator, God if you like, intended me to be. Self-forgiveness is the hardest, but I'm encouraged by the mental silence that is happening more frequently. I think my inner critic is beginning to lose steam, and if the cramp in my hand is any indication, it looks like that I might actually finish this story, for the first time in my life.

I've been a therapy patient since age ten and, frankly, did not expect yesterday's session to yield any new information. Surprise! It is apparent that the self-doubt and sabotage of my adult life is directly related to unresolved feelings of self-loathing, which have been brought to life. Once more, apparently as a result of this writing, revealing the stark fact that despite having been forgiven by most of the individuals and institutions I have encountered, there exists still within me those voices which are revealed not of a separate nature but clearly my own unwillingness to forgive myself of the actions and events now long forgiven, ended and forgotten by everyone but me. My therapist's suggestion that it is time to face these demons, sit with the ensuing feelings, without running away or using food or sex or activity to dull them; is met with disdain and a strong desire to do exactly those things that would prevent facing down the sabotaging head voices.

The breakthrough comes with the realization that it is the running that has created the bumps in the road of recovering myself.

"I'm afraid if I feel these feelings, I will go crazy and die," I say in a pleading voice.

It occurs to me as I speak these words that the truth is obvious. Insanity and death will be the result if I do not stare them down.

For now, I will set this task aside and return to the story. There is still much more to tell.

After leaving Norwalk Hospital, I returned to New York City with a new perspective on why I was the way I was. It had been suggested that I abstain from alcohol and drugs and find support in doing so. I celebrated this notion by toasting it with a rum and coke at the bar in Chelsea that had been my chief source of support for many years. My attitude at the time was that, yes, I was an alcoholic and drug addict, but you would drink and take drugs, too, if you had my life. And now I had this disease that was beginning to kill my friends, so what's the use anyway? I'm going to die and I welcome it!

I met Leon at the Stable Bar, right across the street from the building where I lived with Rick, at the start of the Jamaica trip. Leon was a bright, half-Chinese, half-African American, and he pursued me with an energy that frankly scared the daylights out of me. It would take a few months, but curiosity would get the better of me and, having nowhere else to go, cause me to use the keys to his apartment on East Ninth Street, keys he gave me on our first date, making him, obviously, mad.

It was the start of a love affair that would bring me to my knees in a new and terrifying way as I was introduced to the nightmare world of crack cocaine addiction. The AIDS epidemic would become personal at this time as, one by one, the occupants of the building would die from the disease.

My memories of this time are hazy at best but, as usual, there are a few pivotal points that remain crystal clear to this day.

I am sitting on a pile of trash in an abandoned building on East Thirteenth Street. I would reach up and unscrew the ceiling light which is just above my head, filled with paranoia and anxiety. I scrape the glass pipe, trying to get enough residues to get high.

The other memory is about how the crack story ends. Not a stranger to despair, I have never been in as dark a place as the pit of crack withdrawal. If my mother, whom I loved more than anyone on this earth, were alive, I would have traded her in for a five-dollar hit of a substance that was literally killing me. It was January 5, 1987, 6 A.M. as I walked up Second Avenue from Ninth Street dressed in a white T-shirt, jeans and engineer boots, oblivious to the cold, sweating as if it were August. I needed a fix. I had no money, and had no way to get any. I remember praying to God: "Either kill me or help me to find help."

Plain and simple, without feeling, nor the faith that either event would occur.

Now, I can't prove to you that God exists, but someone somewhere heard me, for by the end of that day, I was admitted to Stuyvesant Square Rehab at Doctors Hospital in the East Eighties where I would begin the long task of rebuilding my shattered life and, even in the midst of the worst tragedies since childhood, experience more love and real joy than I could ever imagine. And now, having committed to paper the horrors for the first time ever, I have made it to the part of my story where the miracles began and the voices in my head are silent.

January 7, 1987, 9 A.M. Group Therapy

I'm 26 years old, homeless, jobless, and penniless. Every bridge to safety has been burned. My emotional state is the same as it was when I stopped growing sixteen years earlier. The group is led by a dynamic woman with a sparkle in her eye and boundless optimism.

Lulled into a false sense of security, the session begins. We are to introduce ourselves and give a short biography. When it gets around to me, I give my well-rehearsed sob story, the one that has gained me many a free drink. It has the desired effect. There is muffled sobbing and sobbing and stunned silence. This is interrupted by the perky voice of the group leader.

"What did he just do to you?" She inquires with that therapeutic tone that says I already know the answer. Can you guess what it is?

Nobody responds, but there is a palpable change in the heavy sadness, and I begin to shift uncomfortably in my chair.

She continues.

"What do you suppose he wants you to feel for him?"

Somebody says softly, "Sorry for him."

"Precisely. That's his whole game. If he can get you to feel sorry for him, he can get what he wants form you."

She is so proud and full of glee. I'm almost stationary on my chair. She addresses me directly.

"And what are you feeling right now?"

I say, "I feel like telling you to go fuck yourself and then leaving."

This is probably the most honest I have ever been.

"Why don't you tell me to go fuck myself and stay?"

Is she serious? I think.

"Can I do that?" I ask meekly.

"Sure, you can say anything you want. You just can't hit me."

I can't remember what I said next, but I always think of Linda Blair's performance in *The Exorcist* as I spit out years of pent-up hostility and emotions. The end result is that I'm sitting in the fetal position, shaking uncontrollably.

My journey home began here.

I

My recovery from alcohol and drug addiction, as well as the diagnosis of my bipolar disorder, and HIV infection, had been a long, slow, and difficult process, filled with much triumph and, yes, a few setbacks.

The AIDS epidemic has proved to be a catalyst for growth in a very profound and intense way. The loss of my childhood pales in comparison to the devastation that this disease had left in its wake.

I became a client of the Gay Men's Health Crisis in New York City in the winter of 1984 where I attended my first support group held in the large conference room of the Eighteenth Street office. It was attended by forty or fifty people, all of whom I would get to know and then watch die. The group room was located next to the hotline office. The hotline was run by a man named Jerry Johnson, a man of boundless energy. He would always stop to say hello whenever I passed him in the hall. One day he said,

"Hey, why don't you volunteer on the hotline?"

His enthusiasm was so mesmerizing that I said yes and spent the next three years voluntarily answering telephones. I would also be introduced to one of the greatest loves of my life, Bruce Woods Patterson. My life finally had purpose as I fought to gain sanity while trying to help educate the general public about this frightening new disease.

When I first sobered up, I had no home, no job, no nothing. Now I was working at a clothing store in Chelsea (for a queen who was so bitchy we called her "Alexis Colby"), volunteering at GMHC, Inc. I attended group therapy six days a week to try and develop some of the necessary life skills that I missed due to my drug-induced haze. My belief in God would grow, and my faith deepen, as my own health faltered and one by one I watched my fellow co-workers and clients die slow, painful, disfiguring and horrifying deaths, and as the living stood by, powerless to stop it, courageously battering an unseen enemy, using every ounce of human spirit and humor to carry on and try to make the loss and suffering less.

An unfortunate by-product of all of this is that I switched my dependency from substance to people, expecting them to somehow save me from what my own doctors assumed was inevitable. I began living in the future, expecting my own painful demise to happen soon, becoming obsessed with each new rash or symptom, trying every new treatment possible, as well as crystal, acupuncture, chiropractic care, Reiki, anything that might keep death at bay since, thanks to my new lease on life. For the first time, I did not want to die, creating no small irony.

Just to complicate life further, I fell in love. Bruce Patterson came to work on the hotline as the assistant coordinator, and I was immediately attracted to his positive attitude and adorable smile. A native Californian, he also believed in alternative medicines I had never even heard of. I now possessed an open mind, born of desperation, though I must admit that I snickered to myself as he cleaned my aura with his hands, a set of crystal patterns beneath the mattress of our bed.

Unfortunately, as I had made much progress emotionally, I still had a long way to go. I put enormous pressure on him for attention, expecting him to calm every new fear, and then resenting him for not being super-human. He was dedicated to his job and was a loving, coaxing partner, but I was still damaged and oblivious to how badly I felt that the work I had done on myself was enough, and blaming him for falling short of my overblown expectations for time and energy.

Bruce's mother became ill and he flew to Alaska to be with her, arriving just in time to say goodbye, because she died a few days later. While he was away, Jerry Johnson, who had been fighting lung cancer, broke down in my arms and cried. This concerned me for he had been a pillar of strength, and I had never seen him break down about anything. He said he was going home, and I told him I loved him and would call him later. After my hotline shift ended, I walked home, and after talking to Bruce, I went for a walk. When I returned to the house, there were three messages on the answering machine:

"This is Jerry Johnson's neighbor. Jerry's lying dead in the hall. I don't know what to do. Please call me back. Beep."

I was stunned. The second message was from Richard Dunne, the executive director of GMHC:

"Scott, we've taken care of Jerry. I'm at the office if you want to talk. Beep."

The third message was from Kevin Mahony:

"Are you okay? Call me."

I was not okay. I called Kevin. He came over and we decided that we both needed a vacation. He had two tickets to Puerto Rico and, while I should have learned my lesson after Jamaica, I said yes and Bruce said go for it.

We arrived in San Juan and checked into the hotel. After quickly changing into our swimsuits, we headed to the beach. I went to the bar and got Kevin a frozen drink and a club soda for me, still proudly sober, and when I returned with the beverages he asked me to put suntan lotion on his back. It was then that I noticed the KS lesions.

"Kevin, when were you going to tell me about the lesions on your back?" I asked, hurt that he had not told me sooner.

"What lesions?" he asked.

I realized in that moment that he did not know they were there and I tried to backstroke, while he rapidly freaked out.

Within an hour, Kevin was on a plane back to New York City, and I was sitting at a bar drinking rum like it was water.

That night at a bar in the Condado, I met a tall, Midwestern man who asked me if I would like to go on a cruise. Without a thought, I said yes and boarded the *Royal Princess* where I proceeded to drink from San Juan to Antigua, Martinique, Caracas, Curacao, through the Panama Canal to Acapulco. My companion drank as much as I did but that was where our similarities ended.

I returned to New York to find my relationship with Bruce on the rocks, and I ended up back on the Lower East Side of Manhattan, where my drug consumption reached a new height. After awhile I sobered up again and returned to work.

Multitasking Systems of New York is a company founded by two physicians to help people with AIDS find work, the first of its kind in the country. The office was located on West Nineteenth Street and housed its administration as well as a copy, print shop business, run by its clients. I began working as a receptionist, and in a year's time, I was given the job of director of Job Development. What this meant was that I had to find jobs for people who were basically unemployable because of sickness, while creating a national model for the Department of Education in Washington, D.C.

Part-time, flexible hours made the most sense, allowing for treatments and appointments. Although there was still the conflict of earnings affecting people's SST-SSDI benefits and with the cost of treatments, the fear of losing insurance and other entitlements became a problem that still exists.

In spite of its difficulties, it was a very supportive environment. We shared symptoms and fears and became a close-knit family. There was plenty of humor and courage as we talked each other through infections and shared the workload, as our company title suggested.

In 1988, our family began to drop dead. First, Carlos had a seizure and died in the office. Christopher developed brain lesions and died soon after. Tonia, Marcus, Richard were dead within weeks of each other. Work fell apart, literally, and the board of directors fired Executive Director Alice King as a scapegoat. I resigned in protest, because I thought they were out of touch with reality. A week after I quit, my best friend, two ex's, and three more co-workers and the executive director from GMHC died within one week.

My ex-boyfriend, Cal, invited me to go to San Francisco for vacation with him and his mother. I had never been to California's northern part, and I was in awe of this city. It's hard to describe what happens when so many people die so close in time to one another. You begin to grieve the loss of the first person, then the next one dies, and soon grief is piled on top of grief, until numbness sets in and new deaths have no effect at all. At first, when this phenomenon occurred I was tempted to check back in to a psych ward, but my therapist assured me that it was a normal response to multiple losses. Another phenomenon was the appearance of ghosts on every New York street corner. People who looked like people who were dead and gone. Many times I would start to call out a name, then remember, oh yeah, he's dead.

I began attending vigils and ACTUP demonstrations as a way to express my grief and rage. Walking solemnly down Christopher Street with white balloons inscribed with the names of so many, to be released *en masse*, as life went on unnoticing. The sobs and cries of names lifted towards heaven.

The quilt on the Washington Mall and seeing Dennis Tham's panel, unaware that he had died. We will never forget you. Joey Leonte, Kevin Mahoney, Rich Croll, Kevin Madden, Tommy Ontek, Gary Pass, Raymond Jacobs, and too many more to name here.

I decided to move to San Francisco, thinking that somehow I would escape AIDS. I realized how laughable this sounds now. Besides, how do you escape a killer you carry with you? And why wasn't I dead yet? This was a question that would begin to plague me as much as the disease itself. The term "survivor's guilt" began to creep into my therapy (word) sessions.

Around this time, I met a man named Patrick Leach, who I fell deeply in love with. His spirit was boundless, and he possessed an optimism that could not be stopped, at least so I thought. He became my unofficial tour guide of San Francisco, showing me all the sights and hot spots. Unfortunately, he did not share my passion towards him, so my dreams of romance were curtailed, and I had to settle for being a good friend. He was always quick with a joke, and he fought HIV with gusto, both personally and professionally. We became partners in crime, and I never felt freer than when buddy-riding down Fell Street on the back of his motorcycle. We were sitting together one day when I spotted a man I would end up spending the next seven years with.

"You see that guy over there?" I said.

"What about him?"

"That's the guy I'm going to marry."

"I think I know why you want him," Patrick said so smugly that I wanted to punch him.

"Oh yeah? Why?"

"'Cause he looks like me."

Before long, I was seeing less of Patrick and lots of Matthew.

Matthew is unlike any man I ever fell in love with, at least physically. For starters, we are the same age, and he is tall and beautiful, so beautiful, that I was certain he would have nothing to do with me. It's not that I think I'm ugly, but I tend to fall into low self-esteem when encountering my prettier gay male counterparts. I was surprised when he expressed an interest, and before long, we were co-habiting. I can see now that we moved too fast, hindsight being 20/20 vision and all, but at the time I was carried away with the romance of it all, and I was certain I was dying so that any commitment made would be a short-term one.

It was just after New Year's of 1992 when my phone rang. It was Patrick's sister, Deborah.

"Patrick's really sick."

I was stunned. She put him on, and all he kept saying was, "I'm so cold. I can't get warm."

He had PCP, and by the time I arrived at his hospital room at Kaiser, he had slipped into a coma. For the next two days, his friends and admirers came by to pay their respects, as his sister and mom and brothers and myself took turns wiping away the fluids he was pushing from his right nostril. It was obvious to everyone that he did not want to die, as he tossed and turned, fighting the inevitable. His kidneys had failed, and the doctors told us that he would die soon.

I had watched hundreds of people die, but had never actually been present at the moment of death.

It was around midnight when Deborah said, "Go get Mom. It's time."

There were eight of us in the room when he breathed his last. I was holding his feet, watching in awe, as his whole body expanded, and then, as if the air were being let out of a balloon, he collapsed into himself, as a palpable rush of energy filled the room, filling with a light that was not coming from the fixtures. Patrick's family began to pray, and I joined in, not knowing what else to do. What amazed me the most was how beautiful, even radiant, he looked right after that moment of death. His face, relaxed and peaceful, looked younger than it had in life, free from the rage and struggle of fighting this awful disease.

After watching the blood pool in his sides for a while, his brother removed his nipple rings and handed them to me, and though it seemed a little morbid, I was glad to have them as a reminder of his soaring spirit.

Making my way to the Castro Country Club, a sober coffeehouse where Patrick and I would OD on latte and get into heated arguments that would clear the room, I joined our friends in mourning his loss. And then the wave of death began again, as when I'd left New York, one by one the patrons of the club succumbed to the epidemic with no end in sight. DeDe, Bill, Rob, Brick, Garrett, Buddy, and many more as the nightmare continued. And I wondered when I would join the familiar faces in the obituary column of the *Bay Area Reporter.*

Around this time, Matt and I decided to relocate to Provincetown, as moving from coast to coast had become too expensive and employment for Mike was more of a sure thing. He was also a budding fine artist and the town provided ample opportunity for learning and showing work. I was unable to work full-time due to increasing health difficulties, so I turned my attention to volunteering, mostly producing benefits for our local AIDS Service Organization, as well as the Soup Kitchen and the PAAM. This also provided me with an outlet to perform and, for a time, my life was more blissful than it had ever been. Matt and I adopted a dog named Lucky from the Brewster Animal Rescue, and while Matt's art career flourished, I threw myself into project after project, some very successful, some dismal failures, but all of them lessons in growing up. The one benefit of having death constantly breathing down my neck has been that it has caused me to take risks and fulfill dreams that otherwise might have been postponed until they were mere shadows of regret. I recorded an album, sang on the stage, appeared on TV and film, published some writing, and sold a joke for a thousand bucks that ended up being told at the Grand Ole Opry in Tennessee. I've visited everywhere on this earth I've ever dreamed of visiting, and faced my fears head-on. As I look back on my life, I can see the sure hand of some kind of power, God or Goddess if you like, had led me, held me, guided, protected, yes, saved me, from harm and death many times over, often in the form of angels who look just like you and me. I have returned the favor, as an angel to others, in service to that power, though I have no proof.

And now, I've written it all down, at least what has seemed pertinent and this brings me to the close of the story, where I can tell you where I'm at today, what's happening, and what I think I've learned so far.

Matthew and I ended our relationship last year. We remain good friends, a testimony to our maturity and love for one another.

I baby-sat Lucky as often as I can, and he seems unaffected by the breakup as long as there are treats to be had. I still miss being in Matt's arms at night, but I'm learning to hold on to myself in new and exciting ways. I know now that no human being can keep me from dying when the time comes, or make me happy, if I choose to feel otherwise. Thanks to medical advances, I am experiencing more good health this year than I did in the previous ten, and I actually am beginning to have hope for the future. My viral load is undetectable, my T-cells are within normal range, and my depression medications, coupled with regular therapy, are working, as they should.

I've done my best to amend the wreckage of my past, the only remaining amends are financial and in the event that this book sells, they will be the first things I pay off. It was never my wish to cause anyone financial difficulties and even though these debts are with investors who lost their money fair and square, I still feel obligated to make good on their capital outlay.

My struggle with AIDS has taught me many things. The most important one has been courage. Courage to stare death in the face, as well as untold suffering and laughter, knowing in my heart of hearts that love is ultimately stronger than death. Once, on a Salada teabag holder, I read something that has always stuck with me and watching all the men I've known and loved die over the past fifteen years has proved it to be true, time and time again. It said: "The human spirit is stronger than anything that can happen to it." I know this to be true.

This writing has brought a newfound peace to my life by helping me to face some things about myself, which I had been having trouble facing.

Now I am finding self-acceptance in ways I didn't think were possible. I can feel years of self-hatred evaporating, the painful scars of childhood healing, and a new sense of purpose growing inside of me. My own homophobia is being replaced by a new sense of pride. Pride in being a gay man who has survived years of abuse, both by others and myself. I can state today without hesitation that God loves me, just the way he or she created me; that my life is as important as all life and with this comes a newfound compassion for others, as I watch them struggle, young and old, with the same fears I struggle with.

Never, never give up. Love yourselves, and one another, no matter what and as Obi Wan Kenobi said,

"May the force be with you."

At the completion of this writing I was in a state of euphoria that often occurs in the first stage of my manic episodes. I began to run around town, telling people that I had written a book and that "They" were going to make it into a movie. Before long I would be in a full-flight from reality.

These writings are done after my release from Silver Hill Hospital. I began taking a new anti-psychotic drug called Geodon. The effects on my focus and concentration abilities were dramatic. The drug effected my ability to communicate on paper as well, and I discovered writing again. It was at this point that I decided to try and tell the story of my illness. I have included some shorter writings on related subjects here because I was amazed at how much the drug helped me and I wanted to share this with you. Short stories anyway. I hope you find them interesting. At this time I still did not have the patience, balance or mental health to tell my story the way I would have liked to. I was also suffering major setbacks. Medication adjustments, coupled with bouts of psychosis making it impossible for me to complete a manuscript. While Geodon showed great promise, it was by no means a cure all. It would be some time before I achieved enough balance to attempt to tell my story again.

The trouble started when I decided to quit smoking cigarettes. I had tried to stop on many occasions before but this time I had new hope because I was going to be using the drug Wellbutrin, also known as Zyban, and it was being touted on television as a new and effective way to break the nicotine addiction without using nicotine substitutes. Something I had tried in the past and failed at. Oh, I had succeeded for a while. Actually I quit for three years. People would say "You look healthy" when they would run into me after a long absence. I knew that they could tell that I had gained sixty pounds and that I had a double chin. I knew this because I had an uncle who said to me, "Jesus, you got fat!" one summer when I went to visit my cousins who were staying at some cottages in Truro and he, being a man of few words, just laid it on the line. My formerly thirty-two-inch waist was now a thirty-eight-inch waist and I avoided reflective surfaces, preferring the twisting quick evaluation to the profiled one. I think it's how I threw my back out. Eventually, I did the only natural thing. I started smoking again. And that brings me to the whole Wellbutrin mess. Now, mind you, I would like to blame the events that occurred during the summer of 1999 on this particular drug alone, but then there is me, Scott Jordan, the person. I come with a whole collection of problems other than nicotine addiction.

But the flashpoint was quitting smoking so I will start there. Things were going along fine at first. I was taking the drug for a week, just as my doctor had prescribed, and I noticed that cigarettes were starting to taste different when one day I just decided to quit. I had been going to the gym and the pounds were melting off. People started to notice and I began to feel better and better about myself. All in all, my life was beginning to look up. Suddenly, my whole outlook on life just changed. Now, for those of you in the know, Wellbutrin is an antidepressant medication.

So, as I was saying, I was feeling great. Going to the gym, not smoking, eating right, and losing weight (can you imagine, not smoking and losing weight!) when I was offered the opportunity to manage the twenty-fifth anniversary production of Harvey Fierstein's *Torch Song Trilogy* at the Provincetown Town Hall. I guess now would be a good time to mention that I am a semi-retired show business professional. Actually, I had successfully produced many shows in Provincetown in the past so I was sought out by the show's backers to manage this production. Imagine that. They came looking for me. I was riding real high!

In less than four weeks, I would be sitting on a beach juggling glow in the dark rubber balls with a holy Bible opened to Revelations, wearing a neon green-and-purple bathing suit that was too tight. My hair dyed bright red. My diet: pure caffeine and sugar. I hadn't slept in three days. I was waiting for the Mother Ship to land at sunset and our Lord and savior Jesus Christ to take me to heaven. Or at least to come to tea dance with me. It was the fourth time in my life that this had happened. A psychotic break from reality is what they call it in the mental health field. I was still not smoking. My friends were talking to the police and my therapist. They were trying to figure out how to get me to a hospital.

Silver Hill Hospital is located in my hometown of New Canaan, Connecticut. I have known about this hospital all of my life because my mother was a patient there and when I was young, she would take me with her when she went for therapy. I grew up two houses away from its grounds and used to sneak into its main house to buy cigarettes when I was thirteen (no shortage of irony here!). My peers in school referred to it as the "Nut House." My mother preferred to call it the "Funny Farm." Innocuous terms meant to remove the horrible stigma attached to mental illness.

I felt a lot of shame for having had a relative who had been treated there. But then I felt a lot of shame growing up in New Canaan. For one thing, I was gay. They didn't call me that in school. I will spare you the more pedestrian references. Homophobia was the least of my troubles. Mental illness, alcoholism, and the physical abuse and poor sexual boundaries that stem from these diseases are the traumas that haunt and continue to challenge me even to this day.

But back to the story. I went to Silver Hill at the advice of my therapist who said, "Your friends are concerned about you."

I said to him, "What do you think?"

I trusted him, and I was also impressed by the fact that he had shown up at my house on a Sunday when I hadn't called him.

"I think you are very manic and delusional. Several of your friends have called and some have come to see me and they are very concerned about you."

"What do you think I should do?" I was very agitated, since none of them had called. It was at that point that he recommended to me that I go for a complete psychiatric consultation to Silver Hill, which coincidentally was a former place of employment for him. "Okay, I'll go, but I think it's you guys who have the problem." My agitation was replaced with grandiosity.

I remember saying all this and knowing in my heart that I was in deep trouble. I just didn't want to come down. I knew what was waiting for me in the pit. And I was not sure that I could get through that again. I agreed to go to the hospital because I was afraid for my life.

For confidentiality reasons, I can't get into a detailed description of the hospital itself. It is beautiful and serene and I was fortunate to have the connections to afford myself getting into a hospital of good reputation on such short notice. If you have seen movies like *One Flew over the Cuckoo's Nest*, then you know that state hospitals can be horrible, but I must say, for myself anyway, that being mentally ill is so horrendous that as long as you have proper care, it doesn't matter if the grounds are pretty. I digress. I arrived at the office of Dr. Scruffullo (not his real name) and I even noticed that I was agitated at this point. I think by now the reality of what had happened was sinking in. I was also starting to come down.

The doctor entered and offered me a seat. I remember doing my best to try and control my body language but to no avail. The more I would try to remain calm the more agitated I became. I eventually ended up pacing around the small interviewing room as I spouted off the details of my summer in Provincetown to Dr. Scruffullo.

"I think you would benefit greatly from a mood stabilizer," he said.

I drove back to the Cape, my mind going faster than the car and wondered what I was going to do. Should I take this pill? I had taken Lithium, Depakote, and countless other drugs in the past, and they all had made me depressed and fat. Besides that, I had my HIV drugs to contend with. I knew that I had to come down because the whole town was up in arms over my behavior which was beginning to become clear. I was starting to remember and would soon be reminded just how bad my acting out had been. So upon my arrival home, I took matters into my own hands and knocked on my neighbor's door. He was not happy to see me. He was upset, in fact, over my out-of-control behavior. I suggested that we smoke a joint to calm things down. I convinced him that it would be a good idea. I had a long history of self-medicating. It is a common behavior among manic-depressives. I began smoking pot on a regular basis again. This added paranoia to an already fragile mix. One by one, friends came up and let me know how they felt about what they had just witnessed. That was, those of them who were not either too afraid or disgusted or disinterested.

Here is a brief sampling of what was said to me in the weeks after I returned from my full psychiatric work-up.

"Scott, do you remember coming into our store taking off your clothes, leaving them, and then leaving?"

I was at a restaurant with some friends (yes, there were one or two who were still talking to me; Provincetown is a very forgiving community).

"Sort of," I replied sheepishly.

"Well, we still have them if you want them."

I was mortified but I kept on smiling. I have found that it helps to just keep on smiling. It also makes you feel better and it scares people and keeps them at a safe distance.

"My favorite part was watching you roller-blade down the street in your underwear every day. We were wondering whether you were going to be taken out by a UPS truck." I took offense to this because I have been skating since the age of five and have only fallen once since the age of six. Those were my fourth pair of roller blades in three years; I had worn out the last three. I had totally overlooked the fact that I was skating in my underwear.

The marijuana was making me very defensive, and while I was now available for conversation again, I was far from being well. In fact, things were about to take a pretty bad turn because I decided to fill the Tegrital prescription that Dr. Scruffullo had given me. This, mixed with the marijuana, would lead to a much darker psychosis. One that would lead to a much longer stay at Silver Hill.

I started taking Tegrital and kept smoking marijuana. It comes down to the drugs. Of course, legal drugs which are managed by a trained professional along with talk therapy are the preferred treatment for manic-depression. My self-prescribed regimen proved to be a recipe for disaster, not to mention further public humiliation, as I began the pendulum swing in the other direction.

Most of you have been depressed in your lives. I am assuming that you have at least felt sad. Imagine the feeling of sadness. Now multiply it one hundred times and sit with it twenty-four hours at a time. That is depression. That is where my combination of Tegrital and pot smoking were taking me. The mountaintop of euphoria had given way to the abyss and what was emerging was an old demon. Suicidal depression.

It was no stranger to my family or me. My mother, grandmother, and my maternal uncle had taken their own lives by the time that I was fifteen, and I had experienced depression symptoms since that same age. Not to mention the grief and loss of these key people whose struggle I had witnessed. I could not understand then that they suffered from a sickness, one that I would wage a mighty battle with later on in life. And I was perplexed because they were often cheerful, entertaining me with jokes and stories, and when they took their lives it was too much for my young mind to fathom.

The circumstances surrounding my grandmother's and uncle's deaths were eerily similar. They both died by asphyxiating themselves in garages not two houses apart with car engines running. My uncle chose the anniversary of my mother's death. Mother outdid them both. She and her third husband were on a reconciliation cruise to the U.S. Virgin Islands traveling at full speed on the *Europa*. We had seen them off at the dock in New York. I knew something was up because I tried to stow away on the ship and actually delay the ship's leaving. Between that and my mother's jumping, I'm sure the passengers were thrilled with my family. They never found her body. But back to my story.

So I'm sitting in my Provincetown apartment, stoned and coming down from this really bad manic episode and I start to hear voices. They are telling me some really bizarre shit. I figure "Oh well, what do you expect, Scott, you've just had a really scary breakdown, just take the Tegrital and try to relax."

The long and short of it is I end up calling a friend of the family who helps me get into Silver Hill for an extended stay. I arrive at the Acute Care Unit shortly after New Year's Eve in 1999. It is nothing like the hospital I grew up looking at on Valley Road. The idyllic green hills have been replaced by a locked ward. I didn't even know that there was a locked ward. And suddenly I'm on it.

I hate to use words like surreal to describe anything that's happening in a mental hospital, but you must understand that I spent my entire childhood passing by this hospital, sneaking onto its grounds, floating down the river that runs behind it in an inner tube on hot summer afternoons with a group of guys that once included my friends Kevin Ruth, Bill Merikalio, and Rick Moody (he would later write *The Ice Storm*) and now, suddenly, I'm sitting on the deck, the wire cage-covered deck, doing what else, smoking a cigarette, on the inside looking out at the world I had escaped from. My freedom lost for the moment, questioning my future as I began a new struggle with the help of my perky new psychiatrist.

After a short stay at the Acute Care Ward, when I had proven to the staff that I was no longer a danger to myself or to them, I was transferred to the Main House where the more serene settings I fondly remembered from childhood awaited. Here, I would receive visits from my father, sister, and brother, as well as my best friend

William. They would all offer their encouragement and support. I would tell them jokes and entertain them, trying to laugh this latest episode off. Just like all the past ones. I think this is how I protected myself. And the people I love the most.

I should say out of respect to the good doctor that my initial judgments of him were born out of my own discomfort at the time. Had he been wearing the simplest of smiles, any depressed person would have labeled him with some snide title as I did. But as we continued to meet over the next few days, not only did he gain my trust and confidence, but also he built a hope inside of me and a willingness to fight my disease that remains as of this writing. His optimism was infectious. While I never found the courage to ask him about it myself, I began to suspect, the more time we talked, that he might be suffering from some form of mania himself.

After finishing an intake, we began discussing my treatment plan. We both agreed that in the light of my symptoms, my history of hallucinations, both auditory and visual, especially during my severe manic episodes, a mood stabilizer, preferably more than one, was in order. I am also a bipolar of the type who becomes very depressed so we discussed antidepressants. While on the Acute Care Unit, it became clear that because of my racing thoughts and delusions, an anti-psychotic would also be necessary. At first I refused. Anti-psychotic! Really. I mean I am a little hyper and certainly confused—but psycho? I have never hurt anyone in my life. (I was hung up on the definitions from Anthony Perkins' characterization, certain that psychotic meant that you had to be violent.)

I agreed after much haranguing to take a drug called Risperdal because, frankly, the voices in my head were driving me up a wall and I was heading into mania rapidly. I had begun to pace up and down the halls of the ward and this is not a behavior that the nurses and attendants view as acceptable. Especially once you get to about four or five miles per hour. This starts to irritate the other patients and makes it harder for the staff to control everyone. So I agreed to take the drug, heck—I even went into the quiet room willingly. Eventually, I calmed down and was able to get to sleep.

The next morning, the most astonishing thing occurred. For the first time in many, many years, I woke up feeling a sense of peace. I couldn't find out what it was right away. Then it hit me. For the first time in many years, the voices in my head were quiet. That peace I felt wasn't coming from outside of me; it was coming from inside of me. I realized that this was due to the fact that I had taken an "anti-psychotic" medication.

The next months were filled with hour upon hour of group after group discussing every aspect of mental illness as well as daily sessions with my psychiatrist. No stone was left unturned. There was also a dining room where lots of fattening food was served three times a day, and a kitchen where snacks could be found at any hour. Smoking took place outside in the front and the back of the building, also at any hour. I took up both of the pastimes with a vengeance until I had gained an extra fifty pounds and was smoking a pack a day.

While I was happy with the progress of my mind, my appearance and self-esteem were back in a rut. When I spoke to my doctor of my concern over my weight gain, he informed me that it was a common side effect to gain weight from drugs like Risperdal and Xyprexa. I had tried both of these drugs. One of the difficulties, in fact I found out the greatest difficulty in treating manic-depressives like myself, is that we would prefer to self-medicate rather than have to deal with such side effects. I understood this as I tried to hide my ever-expanding waistline under bigger sweatshirts. My appearance was all I had (so I thought) and I had already decided that as soon as I left the hospital, I would stop taking any drug that was making me gain weight.

Group therapy occurred six times a day at the hospital and the subjects varied from day to day, although at the end of two weeks we began to repeat ourselves and return to the beginning. A lot of the stuff was very helpful, but after two weeks I was hungry for individual attention and more knowledge about my condition so I began to spend time at the library, looking at the available literature about bipolar disorder, hoping that I might find some relief. The more I remembered about the summer, the more it sunk in what had actually happened, and the more frightened I became. I hungered now for any and all knowledge that might help me gain control over a brain that had literally turned against me. I had fought HIV for years and was winning the battle (my viral load was undetectable, my T-cells 519) but now I had a new enemy: my brain. I mean it had always been problematic, now it was a potentially fatal flaw, a disruption to my life. I was incarcerated in a mental hospital, one that I had no desire to leave, yet I was well aware that I had only so many days available on my insurance (190) and that I might need them in the future. I had a new battle to fight and the terrain was unfamiliar. I needed information. A strategy.

Of all the books that I read (and I read them all), I think I have to credit Patty Duke's *A Brilliant Madness* for helping more than any of the others. It spoke to me in simple language, from the perspective of another sick person without all the flowery medical jargon that I had found so agitating and confusing in other books. It touched my heart and soul and offered me hope. If Patty could get well and survive and lead a good life, so could I. Still I was disappointed. I realize now I was also still very sick and suffering. I had a long road ahead of me, although I didn't know that then.

"A RELATIONSHIP WITH CIGARETTE"

I remember the first time I smoked a cigarette. Well, actually, I tried to smoke it. I stole a Kool from one of my mother's packs and hid it in my closet. It stayed there for about a year before I could muster up the courage to try and smoke it. I took a pack of matches from my stepfather's bureau and snuck into my closet on one of the occasions when my mother had left me unattended. I was nine years old. The cigarette now very stale, though as a nine year old I did not understand or appreciate such things, represented danger, excitement and above all, adulthood. These things I craved desperately because my childhood was filled with powerlessness and pain, as I witnessed the fatal spiral of my mother's life, while an alcoholic father beat her into further insanity and despair. I stood by helpless, a young man in a small boy's body, watching with rage and frustration as the woman I loved most was battered and abused.

Years of therapy and clear hindsight have everything to do with why I can see myself now, hiding in that closet on Birchwood Avenue in New Canaan, Connecticut, fumbling in the dark, a nine-year-old potential fire hazard, unwittingly embarking on a lifelong addiction.

The experience was probably very similar to every other young smoker's experience. I coughed, and felt sick to my stomach. And it tasted really awful. I was so confused. Everyone around me smoked. My father, my mother, my two older brothers, and just about everyone I idolized on television and film screen. So it made little sense to me that something so foul and nasty was so prevalent. Smoking was a constant in our household. Everyone did it all-day long every day of the week and they all seemed to enjoy it, except for the coughing attacks and the ominous warnings that I should never ever start smoking. This only added to my confusion, for as a young gay child who was already feeling attractions for the same sex, particularly men in leather who smoked, I wanted nothing more than to fit in and smoking seemed to be the hot ticket (excuse the bad pun).

Needless to say, I was so sick from my first attempt to start smoking that I did not try again until I was thirteen years old and in junior high school. Puberty was in full swing and the evidence of my same-sex inclination was apparent to everyone but me. I did my best to hide my effeminacy under macho posturing, and smoking seemed like a natural effect to add, after all every Hollywood tough guy smoked. I studied my older brothers, James Dean, and the Marlboro man, and pretty soon I had their gestures down. Next came the walk and the talk, and before long I could pass for a reasonable facsimile of a straight guy, well at least for short periods of time.

It was at this period of my life that my smoking addiction took hold. Peer pressure coupled with that ever-present desire to fit in caused me to turn to cigarettes as a form of looking and acting cool and manly, so I thought. Before long, I was smoking upwards of a pack and a half a day of Marlboro Reds, which I was stealing from my older brother, who kept a carton in his room. It wasn't long before he caught on and I had to get an older kid to buy them for me. It also wasn't long before my mother and stepfather caught on and I was in big trouble for smoking. They screamed and lectured me about the dangers of smoking, how disappointed they were in me, with an alcoholic beverage in their one hand and cigarette in the other. But they started before they knew it was bad for them and they were too old to stop and none of this made any sense to me, though it does now.

I left home at the age of eighteen and entered the world of leather bars where I could smoke as much as I wanted to, whenever I wanted to, and didn't care that I smelled like a walking ashtray. I smoked pot and drank alcohol now in large quantities. I took whatever drug you gave me then asked you what was going to happen, thinking that somehow I was being brave. Looking back, I think that I just wanted to escape the pain of being gay and different.

Over the past fifteen years, I have let go of all the substances. Smoking has been the most insidious of all my addictions. I have tried the patch, hypnosis, cold turkey, cutting down then stopping, and acupuncture. Once I quit for three years and for the entire three-year period, all I thought about, talked about, and even dreamt about was smoking. Some of my friends even begged me to start again. Eventually, I did.

I remember the day I picked up a cigarette again. I was in New York visiting my friend Mark. He was dying. He had dementia and diarrhea and when I arrived at his house, he was alone without any toilet paper. You can put the rest together. I went to the corner store on Third Avenue and bought toilet paper and a pack of Marlboro Reds. I smoked three of them in rapid succession. I didn't even get dizzy. It was one of the times in my life when I can say that I actually enjoyed smoking very much. Mark died two weeks later. His suffering was over. Mine was just beginning again, for I had re-addicted myself to nicotine and was now smoking again. My lover didn't smoke. My singing voice would begin to suffer and before long my overall health.

Which brings me to the now. After four years of smoking more than ever, a pre-cancerous lesion, smoking pot again, stopping smoking pot again, getting oral thrush, and turning forty, I have just quit again. Will I succeed? I hope so. I am committed to the process and I have the love and support that I need. I also know what I'm up against. All around me, people are still smoking all day long all the time. But I'm not confused anymore. I can be a man and not smoke. I can even act butch if I want to. And smell better. And have more stamina in bed and better orgasms. Who knew? Smoking is a big lie. I'm not falling for it anymore.

"A DAY AT OUTER CAPE HEALTH SERVICES"

The pain in my head is familiar. This does not make it less frightening than the last time it had occurred. It is the by-product of a swelling related to an ear infection. My second in two months. I think it began when I touched my eye while making brunch for some friends. I had raw egg on my hand. My theory is that I am now allergic to eggs. Why not? I am allergic to everything else. Mosquitoes. Pollen. Dust mites. Why not raw eggs? It is just preposterous enough to be plausible. It is the way my life has been going lately. The moon has been in the house of stupid.

My physician assures me that these allergic reactions I am currently experiencing are a new side effect. A result of a jerry-rigged immune system. The creation of modern science. He says that due to advances in HIV medicine, I can now expect surprises like these.

Last week, I was bitten by a bug, a "no see ems" as they are so affectionately called. These small, unassuming flies leave large welts. And with my new and improved immune system, with all its new little allergic quirks, my arm suddenly swelled up like a balloon. At first, I thought that my triceps workout had been really successful. Then I noticed the redness and the burning sensation, the itching, and the fact that my other arm was nowhere near the size of the left one. I reluctantly piled into the car and made the trek to the doctor's office.

"Hi Scott. What's new?" Gwen, the receptionist, was becoming rather nonplused at seeing me without an appointment. I have grown fond of her.

"My arm's swollen up. Something bit me," I said, showing her the arm for affect.

"I'll get you right in," she said. She was so matter-of-fact. I would have had hurt her feelings, but we are family, Gwen and I. We understand each other. We see more of each other than we do our parents. I knew she was just as overwhelmed with patients and didn't have a lot of time to coddle me that day. It was summer in Provincetown. She was busy. Besides, I was really more concerned about my arm and its swelling.

"Scott Jordan." It was my favorite nurse, Kathy, calling my name. Actually, I am being facetious. If I were speaking these words instead of writing them, you would easily pick up on my tone. Kathy and I have a long history of doing battle with one another. To say that we have an adversarial relationship would be like saying that a temperature of 107 would be a slight fever.

She loves to bait me. Lately, I have just been ignoring the bait and killing her with kindness. She doesn't know what to do with this. It makes her horribly uncomfortable and gives me some strange sadistic pleasure.

"You look nice today." I said this with my most convincing actor's smile, hoping that somehow she will be convinced.

"I know what you're up to, smartass," she fired back.

Today, when I show up, it's Kathy again and I see a look of concern on her face as she calls me in. "What's up now?" she says with her usual sarcasm, only tired.

"Swelling in my head," I say, much too scared to make jokes.

The last ear infection left me with hearing loss. I see a specialist on August 31 for a full work-up so that I can be fitted for a hearing aid. My hope is that I will be able to stop saying "what?" to everyone. It has become a mantra. That and "could you repeat that, please?"

I want to scream, but instead I smile and make a joke, ever the gentleman and comedian. I wonder how many people have died from politeness. Fewer and fewer these days. Yesterday, I told my friend Channing, who is one of John Waters' regular actors, and friends that I would like to be introduced to Mr. Waters so that I could tell him how much I loved *Serial Mom*. If you haven't seen it, it's about a mother who starts to off people with bad manners.

Lately, I feel that way. It has a lot to do with my upbringing.

And the fact that I am clinically insane from time to time. I just took what is classified as a major tranquilizer and I am waiting for it to take effect. Of course, true to form, I washed it down with a diet Coke and a brownie so who knows what will happen?

"Scott Jordan." This time it's Susan, the first nurse who ever saw me at Outer Cape, over ten years ago.

"How's it going?" She is sincere. Hard to read.

"Good. Challenging. I am becoming one person after being many for most of my life. Not sure I like it."

She smiles as if she understands.

"Is that what you want?" She looks concerned. "I like being lots of different people," she says, smiling.

She doesn't understand.

"ABOUT AUGUSTITIS"

Augustitis should be classified by the AMA as an actual disease. Now I am not a doctor. I am not sure by what criteria an illness is measured. Fever, chills, rash, and the like. I think that in that case Augustitis would definitely qualify. Then, of course, there are the behaviors. They are perhaps the most heartbreaking. People suffering from this condition need our compassion. They are going through a very trying time. I'm beginning to visualize a telethon with Enya performing.

The other day, I watched a normally polite and kind individual, whose identity I will protect in the interest of confidentiality, snap in line at the A&P.

"For God's sake, lady, would you move your *%$# cart, I haven't got all day," he barked. Once an outstanding example of a seamless passing through a Provincetown season, he barely resembled his former self. Now, before me, stood a haggard, unkempt, harpy; shrill, shrieking at anyone who would listen. No one would listen. "Her goddamn cart is taking up the entire lane. I can't take it anymore."

This was the third incident I had witnessed in the same week. It was a painful transition to watch. A formerly kind and patient citizen of our town, stricken by this senseless malady, as so many are when the sun begins to wane at the end of our summer.

"Did you hear about poor Ryan?" I strained forward, dropping my plastic box of blueberries on the linoleum floor, sending the overripe berries shooting everywhere, bending down to pick them up while careful not to miss a word. "He went off and just let her have it. Told her to just go fuck herself right there in the post office. You could have heard a pin drop. Go fuck yourself he said, just like that, plain as day like he was reading a shopping list or something. You just couldn't believe your ears. I almost fell over myself when I heard it . . ."

I was beginning to wonder if the queen telling the story was going to take a breath when the store manager came over and began helping me pick up my berries. "Having fun, are we?"

"Is it that obvious?" I was enjoying it all very much. He helped me pick up the rest of my fruit and we took a moment to reflect on the summer's casualties.

"Did you hear about poor Ryan?"

"I was just getting bits and pieces of it in the line. From what I understand, he came apart pretty bad. What did you hear?"

"Something about him being at the A-House last night and being hit by some drag queen with a tiara. The other drag queen fired back with his purse and then he just lost it. Lost it completely. I mean, what's happening to these queens? Have they gone mad?"

"It's Augustitis," I said. Last night at work, Dan asked me to measure his nose.

I began this last writing approximately three years after leaving Silver Hill Hospital. By now the medicines as well as talk therapy and my support system were having the desired affect and I was feeling better than I had in my entire life. I decided to try and write my story one last time, this time focusing on manic-depression.

There is some repetition, though I did my best to "mix it up" and make things new and interesting. If you can hang in there until the epilogue I think you will find a message of hope.

INTRODUCTION

I am not a writer. I thought that I should mention this right away so that there won't be any surprises. I am, like most of the manic-depressives I have met, a talker, and a fast one at that. I can promise that I will do my best to make this an interesting read. I barely completed high school and, if it weren't for spell check, I would not be able to spell. It is, in fact, a small miracle that this writing is in your hands at all because I also hate to type. You see, I am not very good at typing and this work has been produced through the old-fashioned, hunt-and-peck method. You may be asking yourselves why the hell this guy writes this, then, if it was such a hassle, and if he is so under-qualified.

I will explain. Three years ago, I was hospitalized for a very severe episode of mania. While a patient at a Connecticut mental hospital, I read every available book in the library about bipolar disorder and was disappointed by most of them. Now, please, don't get me wrong here. I do not presume to think that I can write a better one. My disappointment was with the way they spoke to the reader. A lot of them were written in complicated medical language. Many of the books spent a great deal of time explaining what manic-depression was, going into the details of its symptoms, but very few talked about how to cope with the daily problems that arise out of being a bipolar disordered person! Only one, Patty Duke's *A Brilliant Madness*, in which she shared her personal experience, had the effect of offering any real comfort. I want so much to be liked, but frankly, I am going to have to run the risk of being criticized when I say that most of the available literature does nothing to actually offer any real help to the sufferer of manic-depression.

They all do a great job of describing the illness but fall way short in assistance or suggesting how to cope outside of recommending that you contact certain support groups which, I suppose, is fine if you are able to travel great distances.

When I pointed this out to my psychiatrist, he suggested that I write my own book. I remember being annoyed at the time. I presented my dilemma to many of the staff and each time they suggested I write a book. I continued my search for literature after leaving the hospital, combing bookstores from the U.S. to Canada and always finding the same books that were in the hospital library. Over the next three years, I would learn a great deal about living with my illness. I understand now what my caregivers where trying to get me to do. They felt, that my personal experience would comfort someone the way that Patty Duke's comforted me at a time when I needed it most. Living with bipolar disorder is a matter of life and death. Truly a matter of life and death. Chances are—if you are holding this book in your hand—you already know this on a very personal level and are searching for the help as I did. I pray that you find in these few pages some peace of mind in knowing that at least you are not alone.

I believe that if you do what I have done and continue to do, you will get the same results or at least a similar one. I equate it to baking a cake. If you use the same ingredients and bake at 350 degrees, you get a cake. It's that simple. Simple, but not easy; in fact, if may be the hardest thing you ever do in your life. I can assure you that it will be easier than living with suicidal depression and mania.

Whatever the case, I appreciate you taking the time to read my effort. I do believe that I have found a way to live with manic depression. I have known the pain of suicidal thoughts and feelings. I have also experienced horrifying manias and psychotic episodes. Today, thanks to advances in modern medicine and rigorous therapy and personal dedication, I also know serenity, peace, balance, and great joy. I have found a solution to my illness.

Scott James Jordan

March 2002

I remember my mother's depressions. She would lie in bed during the day and ask me to come over and lie with her. I was six years old at the time. I would climb into bed with her and snuggle up. She would ask me to play with her hair. As a child, I knew that something was wrong but could not fathom the depth of what was happening. At other times, she was wildly happy. I would long for those times when her sadness struck. Many times she would rage, and I feared her during those times, though often her anger was directed at my brothers and father and stepfather. I was her baby. She was my world.

My brothers began to do drugs and act out. The violence in the house escalated. I became more and more fearful. My grandmother committed suicide, though at seven I didn't exactly understand what that meant. My mother seemed to come unglued at that point, acting stranger and stranger. She would spend time in a special hospital. The same hospital I would eventually receive the help that would save my life. Mom would not be so fortunate. She would not be able to find an answer to the complicated puzzle that is manic-depression. She would jump off an ocean liner on a reconciliation cruise with her third husband before anyone or anything could help her find the balance that I enjoy today. Her body would never be found and I would never fully recover from the loss. Five years later, her younger brother, my Uncle David, would take his life, in a garage next to where my grandmother had done the same not so long ago. As I looked around me, I saw adults and siblings consuming drugs and alcohol in large quantities and I wondered. Would this happen to me? Would I kill myself also?

My nickname is Scooter. My grandfather named me this because I was a hyperactive child. I never stopped. I awoke before sunrise and I wanted to stay up past my bedtime and I never stopped talking. I talked incessantly. They called me precocious. I ran very fast and it was hard to catch me. I laughed easily and I loved sugar; in fact, I lived on it, refusing to eat little else. Sugar-coated cereals; Captain Crunch, Cocoa Puffs, and Fruit Loops were my favorites and my sister complained that I always smelled of cereal. My other favorite food was French toast with lots of syrup. Donuts were a special Sunday treat and cupcakes sent me reeling with pleasure. Of real food, I would only eat hamburgers and fries and little else. My mother would become frustrated with me at times because all that I wanted to eat was sweets. I don't recall eating a green vegetable until after she died. All the sugar fueled my hyperactivity. This would be followed by the inevitable crash with tears, being sent to my room and often a fight with my brother. Almost immediately I would begin talking and my brother would punch me in the face to try to shut me up. Even at an early age, I sensed that I was different from my siblings. My sister would joke that I was adopted. I believe that the first signs of chemical imbalance were evident at a very early age.

After my mother's death, my father gained custody of the three of us and we moved in temporarily with my Aunt Joanne and Uncle Alfred. They had three children of their own and a large dog so you can imagine that it was a tight fit. My aunt and I immediately went to war over my eating habits. She came out on top, being the larger and stronger adversary. I fought a hard battle, but I was no match. It was also at this time that my sensitive nature became apparent. I would cry at absolutely everything. I think most of this behavior was written off to the fact that my mother had just died, but I can assure you that it continues well into my forty-first year.

My aunt and uncle did their very best to make us feel welcome, but the house was just too small so we moved with my dad to a home close to town and it was just the four of us now. My older brother, Jeffrey, took off to Georgia to play drums with a rock group. He was ten years older than me and had a different father. The house on East Avenue quickly become a party house because my dad was working three jobs to support us, and the lack of adult supervision after my oldest brother had left brought immediate trouble. Pot was the primary culprit and my middle brother, Stephen, the chief suspect. I continued my love affair with sugar because I was still too young to get involved with drugs and alcohol, and I had an aunt, my Aunt Mary, who dropped by every day to mostly complain that no one was taking proper care of us.

My father's competency as a parent came into question after too many run-ins with the police for my brother and the next thing I knew I found myself living with another aunt and uncle, this time completely separated from family. I remember becoming very depressed during this time because my new guardians did not allow me sugar, were very strict, and when my father would visit on weekends, I would cry and beg him not to leave me with my aunt and uncle. My uncle used to give me back rubs and then put rubbing alcohol on me which burned my skin, and they had plastic on their furniture, and it was a nightmare. My mother had just died and I missed my father and sister and everyone seemed to think that they knew what was right for me, yet no one would give me any sugar. I slipped into what I believe was my first depression in hindsight. I also began to experience delusions and by this time had become an experienced pathological liar. I was too meek to actually rebel against my aunt and uncle so I played with their heads instead. It was the only way I had to express the rage that was beginning to build inside of me towards the world and God for taking my grandmother and mother, and now separating me from my family.

My father would eventually remarry and we would be reunited as a family. My new stepmother would be ill-prepared for the mental illness which my brother and I will bring to the household, but thanks to alcohol, it will take a while for things to come to a head. I need to state here that it would be impossible for me to write all that has happened to me in my life so I will be skimming over the events that befell me during my adolescence. I could probably fill volumes fleshing out the other characters in my life story, but there is a lot of ground to cover and, in fairness to them, I will let them write their own books should they so choose. I would like to try to stick to my development as a manic-depressive, if at all possible.

As puberty began, I became increasingly energetic and overly talkative to the point where I was disruptive in my classes and an irritant to my friends and family. My stepmother and I were at odds and she would often say, "Why don't you go outside and do something with yourself!" She could not stand in my presence. I did not understand why. I was also emotional, still prone to crying outbursts, which she found very offensive.

Drug and alcohol use began to play a regular part in my life and it was also at this time, around my thirteenth birthday, that I began to be molested by a friend of the family. He was a thirty-five-year-old man whom my parents trusted and with whom I would spend the next three years being sexually abused by. He would teach me the skills that I would need to run away to NYC when my drug use had reached its peak and the abuse from my stepmother had become unbearable.

I ran away to NYC and discovered the gay bars of Manhattan's West Side. Suddenly the center of attention, I began to consume larger and larger amounts of drugs and alcohol. Cocaine, marijuana, and any pill that I could get my hands on helped me to feel good and regulate my energy. My energy was always a topic of conversation. I always had tons of energy. I was the guy who would work three double shifts in a row and then go out dancing. I could go on very little sleep, consume massive amounts of substances, and never seem to tire. But my integrity was another story entirely. I rarely had enough money to pay for all the drugs so I usually took what I needed. This eventually began to cause me problems socially. That and the fact that as my energy became manic, I would become delusional and say things that were flat-out lies or at the very least, amusing fabrications. It would take increasing amounts of substances to get high and my life was heading in circles. I needed to clean up my act and I knew it. One day, while tripping on LSD in Times Square, I decided that I should join the navy. Just like that. Join the navy. So I walked into the little glass booth that is conveniently located in the middle of Times Square and I joined. The next thing I knew I was sitting on a plane heading for Great Lakes, Illinois. I was thinking "This will cure me."

Here's a little free advice. Don't join the navy while tripping on acid. It may seem like a good idea at the time but I can assure you when you come down, you'll wish you hadn't. This was the very situation I found myself in as I did push-up after push-up surrounded by many young homophobic men in basic training camp. I did my best to conceal my gayness, but I am one of those gay men who live right on the edge of gay: A mixture of Harrison Ford and Paul Lynde, if you could imagine such a creature. It was taking all of my energy to keep my gayness suppressed as I was put through the paces of military training. I did my very best out of fear for my life and, fortunately, there were a few recruits who were even more effeminate than I was so I often could count on the spotlight of homophobia being shown in another direction. Still, I never felt safe and the macho posturing was wearing me out. There was something else that was wearing me down even faster. I had not had alcohol or drugs, outside of coffee and cigarettes, for thirteen weeks. This was the first period of official detoxification since I had started using at the age of thirteen. I was feeling physically fit, but I was becoming increasingly talkative and noticeably irritating to my company. It became harder and harder for me to control my energy and my gayness was beginning to show through my defenses as more and more negative comments were aimed in my direction.

As I look back, I can see that my thinking became seriously delusional around this time, too. I became involved in religious activities and decided that I would turn straight. God would heal me of my homosexuality. I had already figured out who else in the company was gay, and I had bonded with one of the men whose goal was to change his sexual identity. We spent hours pouring over the Bible and he assured me that if I really wanted to, I could change. So every night I prayed and I prayed. I went to church and I prayed. I sang in a makeshift navy gospel choir and I prayed. I felt increasing emotionalism and was certain that Jesus was answering my prayers. I had so much energy. I talked so much that I was frequently told to shut up by other sailors. I lived on caffeine and nicotine because they were the only two substances that we were allowed in boot camp. I read Revelations with a vengeance and prayed for the second coming of Christ. I was slowly losing my mind. One night, we all went down to watch the movie

Superman with Christopher Reeves, and I decided that the movie was really a story about Jesus. Then I realized how much I looked like Christopher Reeves. How much I had survived in my life and how I had just healed myself of my homosexuality and it dawned on me that I actually was superman. I was the second coming of Christ!

I decided not to tell anyone. I thought that there must be a reason that God, my Father, had chosen to have me appear to the world as a formerly gay guy from Connecticut who was now in the navy in Great Lakes, Illinois. It's funny now. It felt totally real to me when it was happening. If you suffer from manic-depression, you know exactly what I am talking about. You have probably had an experience with mania.

My first official weekend leave took me to Kenosha, Wisconsin, where I ended up drinking and smoking pot. After being AWOL, I returned to the base with some cockamamie story that I had gotten drunk and married my girlfriend. I suppose a tattoo would have been a nice touch but I did not think of that at the time. I figured that this was the kind of story my company commander would want to hear, though I remember him not believing me, even though I had gone to the trouble of purchasing a cheap wedding ring. A slap on the wrist and it was back to work. The outcome of drinking and pot smoking was that it slowed down my mania somewhat, although my thinking could still be classified as delusional. In hindsight, it was just a Band-Aid, for the real show was about to take place as we graduated from basic training and moved over to the Naval Training Command on the other side of the base.

After signing up for hospital corps school and being transferred, all of one hundred feet, I began drinking again in earnest. This time it would be beer. Somehow, I ended up with alcoholic hepatitis and I asked for an emergency leave so that I could tell, get this one, the mother of my child-to-be that I was sick and that the unborn fetus was possibly endangered. I said that news like this had to be delivered in person and they granted the leave. The next thing I remember was being AWOL again, this time in Harlem, after smoking a joint that was laced with angel dust with some other sailors on the run. I turned myself in and found myself housed comfortably at the Brooklyn Naval Yard and before long found myself back in Great Lakes.

After another wrist slap and fear of serious disciplining, I decided to straighten up and fly right. When I returned to the naval base, I figured that I should do everything right. There was only one problem: I was losing my grip on reality. Now I am going to try my best to describe exactly what happened during this time. I felt a heightened sense of awareness. Colors were brighter and sounds were sharper. Everything seemed more alive. At first, I thought that the drugs I did in New York were having a lasting effect, but I was completely sober at this point. I began to think that the television was trying to communicate with me and that there was some sort of message in coins and paper money that had to do with God. I began to walk over to the naval hospital at night and take the elevator to the top floor and sit cross-legged, looking out the window and certain that at any time the Mother Ship could arrive to take me home. I began to hear mumbled voices—voices that I was certain belonged to aliens, gods, and my dead relatives. They all told me to run to the top of the hospital and meet the Mother Ship. The noise in my head reached a fever pitch until finally I did just that. I was sitting in my room with my roommates. I don't recall their names, but I do recall that they were trimming each other's hair and I suspected that they were gay. Wearing just my underwear and one sock, I stood up and walked out the door and down the hall. My whole body was vibrating at this point and I felt a singleness of purpose. To get to the naval hospital. The hospital was situated across the river from the hospital corps school barracks where I presently was, and I had mapped out my route for the past three nights, though on these occasions I wore the navy uniform. The barracks were co-ed: men on one side, women on the other, with a lounge for socializing in between. I made my way downstairs and entered the lounge and found it to be full of my fellow corpsmen and women. They made a path for me as I walked through and headed for the door towards the back of the room. No one seemed to notice or care that I was almost naked, something that only fueled my delusion that I was on a mission from God to go and meet an alien spaceship carrying my dead mother.

Opening the back door, I walked out onto a walkway and headed for the hospital. I was moving at a normal walking pace and as I turned the corner, one of the ground watches happened to notice me and shouted for me to halt. I did what anyone in my condition would have done at this point. I started running as fast as possible for the hospital; I mean, after all, I had a ship to catch and no one was going to make me late. At this point, I remember being chased by one and then two men as I entered the lobby of the hospital. I figured that if I stopped to take the elevator that I would be caught, so I opted for the stairs. There was another watch asleep at the front desk, and he woke up as I entered the stairwell and joined in the chase. Before long, I was cornered on a stair landing by four men in dark navy uniforms and things had taken a nasty turn. Every time they tried to subdue me, I would deck one of them. I was very impressed by this new ability, for most of my life I had felt only fear when encountering any physical confrontations. I have since learned that when I am manic, fear disappears. In my delusional state, these men in black were evil and were trying to stop me from reaching the Mother Ship. They had to be stopped. I decked all four of them and headed up the stairs where I was met by two officers in white uniforms. In my delusional state, they were angels working for the Mother Ship. When they asked me to calm down, I did as they said immediately and went with them willingly. The next stop was the emergency room where I was asked a lot of questions. I answered the questions with song lyrics and Bible passages along with a lot of other smart-alecky remarks that I found very amusing, and no one else laughed at. When they asked me who was president, I gave the wrong answer, knowingly, and when it came time to sign the admitting forms, I signed three different names, one of them my father's. I watched as I did this and, looking back, I remember thinking at the time "something's wrong with me." This was the first time during the episode that reality crept in. I also remember feeling euphoric and having a sense that I would finally get to see the Mother Ship.

What I got to see was the inside of my very first psychiatric ward. It would be the introduction of a lifetime of medication and self-talk and fellow sufferers. It would also take years, as you will see, for me to believe that I was mentally ill. It was much easier to believe that I had special powers. It was a much happier scenario to think that I was the by-product of an alien human encounter. It was less painful than the truth—that I was seriously mentally ill, that there was no Mother Ship coming.

The psych ward at the Great Lakes Naval Hospital was like every other ward I would visit over the next twenty-two years. The pale, green walls were painted to have a calming effect on the patients and the "Quiet Room" was the same as its many counterparts. It was also the first stop on my tour. I was becoming agitated again when it became apparent to me that I would not be going up on the hospital roof. I was given a pill to take, which I later found out was Thorazine, and I took it reluctantly, suspicious now of everyone and sure that I was being prevented from my mission. As the pill took effect, I slowly began to realize that I was on a crazy ward and that there was obviously a great mistake being made. I still wasn't ready or able to believe that I was delusional for my other reality was too real.

I fell asleep eventually, and when I awoke, my first thoughts were about escape. I had to get to the roof of the hospital somehow. I decided that the best thing to do would be to play it cool and then make a run for it as soon as the opportunity presented itself. I had watched enough television to know that this might work so I settled myself down and waited for someone to come and talk to me. The door opened and a navy nurse came in and asked me the same questions that were asked in the emergency room. I answered them correctly this time, knowing that I would need to control myself if I hoped to escape. It worked. I was led out of the little padded room and into a larger barrack-type room that was bustling with activity and people. As we walked past the nurses' station, it became clear to me who was in charge and who was a captive. In my mind, I did not see the other people as patients. I assumed that they all had missions and were being held against their wills as I was.

I was led to a bed with a night table and given soap and a washcloth. I was told that I would be seeing a doctor in a short while and that I should wash up. I remember thinking "a doctor, what the hell do I need to see a doctor for?" followed by great anxiety. What would they do to me? Would they perform experiments? I had to escape as soon as possible. I went to the bathroom and washed up and then I met the other captives.

Brian was Irish, he spoke well with a fake accent anyway and I pretended not to notice. I told him my story about the Mother Ship and how I had to get out of here and all. He listened intently and then announced that we were long-lost brothers and we should leave together. That we were on the same mission. He then introduced me to the other people on the ward who were on the same mission. It turned out to be almost everyone, except for a couple of people who were on so much Thorazine, all they could do was sit there and drool. I was so happy to know that I wasn't alone. I began to talk wildly about my mission to anyone who would listen. Whenever a nurse or a psych tech was around, I would clam up and talk about normal things. They were the enemy now and they mustn't learn of my plan. Now it was our plan for I would help everyone escape. Brian and I spent hours talking in private about God and Armageddon and spacecraft just to make sure we were on the same page. We even took the same medication that our captors were giving us. We must be brothers! At night, the nurses (I'm sure I called them something else, I just can't remember what) would give me Loxitane to put me to sleep. I hated this pill. It made me very sad, brought me way down, and made me think of dying. The day after, I felt groggy and unclear. I decided that the only way to succeed would be to stop taking these drugs they were giving me. After lining up for our meds, I would slip mine under my tongue, go to the bathroom, and then spit them out in the toilet. After doing this for a few days, I decided that I must tell the others. I was certain that if they didn't stop taking the drugs, they would be kept prisoners forever and we would never escape.

After spreading the word around the ward of the diabolical plot that was afoot, the others joined in and began to follow my lead. What I didn't realize at the time was that most of them were being treated for conditions that, like myself, merited some form of sedation. Within a few days, the ward became a very busy place and the quiet room was seeing a great deal of action. I remember the look on my doctor's face when I informed him that I was aware of the plot to control us, was no longer taking my medication, and had convinced the others to stop taking theirs. He was up and out of his chair before I had finished my last sentence. After informing the nurses of my confession, it then became standard practice that we all showed what was under our tongues after receiving our meds every day.

Eventually, the medication, as well as therapy and doctor's visits, began to take effect on me and I slowly returned to reality. I still did not want to believe that I was mentally ill. The experience that I had just been through seemed so real, but now that my energy and mood were returning to normal, it was hard to argue with the facts. I was also embarrassed and depressed. Everyday life was extremely uninteresting when compared with the colorful and delusional world I had just inhabited. My diagnosis was "transient mental disorder manifested by drug and alcohol abuse." My sister, a nurse, joked with me by saying, "What does that mean actually, that it comes and goes?" We both thought that it was funny and, at the time, I was far more interested in laughing at my circumstances than in taking them seriously.

I was honorably discharged from the navy under medical conditions and felt relief and disappointment at the same time. I had sort of hoped that the service would have straightened me out (in more ways than one) and now I found myself back on square one. I returned home to Connecticut and before long, I was back to drinking and using drugs. I spent almost every night out drinking with my friend Cynthia. We would get as drunk as our money would allow, and often I would pass out at her house. Not realizing that alcohol was a depressant, I became more and more depressed as I lost a couple of jobs, and ended up living with my mothers third husband. The man who I thought had pushed her off of the ocean liner all those years ago. Things came to a head quickly one Easter Sunday as I stumbled into the choir room of the local Methodist church, where I had just given a very hung over performance, and was confronted by the choir director who also happened to be my former high school music teacher. He was angry and I was clueless "What is it going to take" He was shouting and poking me in the chest with his finger. I just stared at him in shock. "What are you talking about?" I sort of knew, but I was really hung over and I didn't quite get it. "How drunk and fucked up do you have to get? How many times do you have to fall on your face before you see that you are wasting your life?" His words cut right trough me and I stood there as if I had been slapped hard in the face. I rescpected this man, even loved him and in that moment I felt completely ashamed. He walked away from me in disgust and I headed home not knowing what to do. I spent the night drinking alone in my room and the next day I woke up feeling more lonely and miserable than I had ever felt. I called my former teacher up and I asked him what he thought I should do. "Call Norwalk Hospital Alcohol Treament center. They can help you." There was tenderness again in his voice. I picked up the phone and called the hospital and the next day I found myself sitting in a small room with a woman named Nancy discussing my drinking, honestly for the very first time.

I ended up in an alcoholism treatment center, the first of many, and for the first time in my life I addmitted that I was an alcoholic and drug addict. It was pretty easy to admit that I had a problem. The real dilemma would occur when time would pass and my mania would surface. I was sober and living in Boston when this happened the first time. Ten months had passed and everything was going well. My overall health had improved. I was working and living on Beacon Hill. I was attending various meetings of twelve step groups and had delveloped several close friendships.

Answers to questions about myself that I had asked for many years were being answered in therapy. Things were great. Around this time I developed a rash on my arms that wouldn't go away. I went to Mass General Hospital and was told that I had swollen lymph nodes. They did some blood tests and informed me that they thought I might have this new "Gay Disease" that was being seen in NYC and San Francisco. I had rececently been in New York. Panic ensued. I became more and more agitated. Drinking cup after cup of coffee, I slowly lost touched with reality as I stopped sleeping. This particular episode of mania stands out for a number of reasons. It was the first time that I cut my own hair and drew on my clothes. I also drew pictures on the walls of my apartment. At the time I couldn't afford a television so I just drew on on the wall. Then I drew an arrow pointing to the phone and wrote" phone" in parenthesis next to it. On my clothes were spirals and arrows and outlines of my genitals. It was at this point that people began to shy away from me. (Years later while in Manhattan I saw a woman who was clearly having a manic break and she had drawn the same symbols on her clothes that I had drawn on mine years earlier.)

To make matters worse, if that were possible, I worked at a coffee shop. Drinking coffee all day, sometimes working double shifts. My boss loved me until I started to draw on my clothes and say that the greek gods were talking to me through the TV I drew on my wall. For I while I thought that there was a porthole from my apartment to the coffee shop were things would just appear. I would set things in the cabinet under the cash register and when I got home they would be on the counter. I was certain they were being teleported there. During a later episode in Provincetown I was convinced that My SAAB was washing my clothes. I would open the hatchback and there would be folded clothing. Obviously I had put it there and forgot that it was my doing. In mania things get going so fast that I start to lose time. As my mental state began to worsen and my mania became severe, I noticed that people were avoiding me, or worse they would express concern for me, which would cause me agitation. I lost my job and now I spent my time walking all over Boston wearing increasingly more bizarre outfits.

I began to wear make-up and the voices in my head were telling me that I was on a mission (unfortunately they were never clear what the mission was exactly).

Eventually, I got on a train and headed to Connecticut. For I had decided that the answers to the mission had to lie in my childhood.

I arrived in New Canaan and proceeded to terrorize the town for a period of forty-eight hours. I started out by going to my favorite twelve-step group. One of the facets of a full-fledged mania episode that has always fascinated me is the ability to control it at times. What I mean by this is that I could make myself settle down if I so willed it. I would notice that I was going too fast and that it was unnerving the people around me so I would tell myself to slow down and I would. This, of course, added to the denial that I had control over the brain chemical disaster that was actually occurring. I really thought that I was not only controlling myself, but by the time my mania was in this stage, I also thought that I was controlling the weather and the earth's rotation. After attending the meeting and interrupting people and causing quite a stir, I headed into town and dropped in on all the jobs I had held during my school years. One in particular, at a deli, found me jumping over the counter and then running out and onto my next stop. I retraced my entire childhood going to all of my schools from grade school to junior high to high school. At some point in the day, the police were called to investigate because I was beginning to frighten people with my energy and the fact that I was not making any sense in my speech. I showed up at my father's house at about midnight and he was so scared he slammed the door in my face and told me to go get help. I went from his house to the police station. I announced to them that I was the guy they had been looking for all day and then I called my sponsor from the twelve-step group and we headed down to the local emergency room. When we got to the hospital, I decided that I didn't want to be committed, that I wanted to go back to Boston. So when the psychiatrist came down to see us and he said, "So what seems to be the problem?" I just refused to talk. My sponsor was livid. I can't say I blame him but you have to understand that at this point I still didn't acknowledge that I was a very mentally ill young man. I thought that I was an alien on a mission from the Greek gods and awaiting instructions. I had no idea that I was seriously manic-depressive. My voices were real.

My sponsor, in his frustration, asked me where he should take me. I said that my Aunt Barbara would probably let me spend the night and he drove me to her house. She said sure, one night would be fine. She called my father the next day and they had a screaming match. He came and picked me up and the next thing I knew I was back on a train for Boston. This time I was convinced that New York was hell and that Boston was heaven and I was on my way to complete my mission. My psychosis was deepening and I was beginning to become paranoid and agitated, which is usually the last phase of my mania before I crash and burn. I arrived in Boston and decided that the best thing for me to do would be to go to Provincetown. As soon as I got to Provincetown, I walked into a bar and I drank. This put a stop to my mania but it also caused me to lose the sobriety that I had worked so hard for. I also came down hard and fast from my delusions and I began to drink and smoke pot again. Within weeks, I wanted to kill myself.

I was admitted once more to Doctors Hospital on Manhattan's upper east side. This time it was apparent to me that there was something else wrong with me than just substance abuse.

I returned to my sober life in New York, though naturally my friends at this point were a little skeptical about my chances of success. I had fallen too many times for most of them and I knew that I would have to prove myself. There were three—Joe, Yvonne, and John—who were still willing to take a chance on me and in the early days of my recovery, they chaperoned me around from meeting to meeting until I got my sea legs.

As for myself, well I was dumbfound as to how I had ended up on my ass again, and the strange thing about the severest part of the manic episode would be that once it ended, I pretty much forget it had happened. I mean, I had enough recall to remember cutting my hair and drawing on my clothes and talking nonsense in a general way, but the experience was a total blur mainly because everything happened so damn fast. I also felt so much shame for the experience that I wanted to distance myself as far from it as possible, and yet it lurked right beneath the surface of my personality. A few too many cups of coffee and I would start talking nonsense, which would usually cause whomever I was with to suggest that I call it a night. It was around this time that I was first introduced to lithium. My experience with it was simple. It slowed me down and caused me to gain weight, so I stopped taking it. Next was Depakote. Same thing. I was terrified I was being slowed down because it meant only one thing to me. Depression. Like my mother and grandmother and uncle before me, I suffered from suicidal depression. I was certain that I would take my life if I didn't fight the sadness and despair I felt when my energy dropped below a certain level. I had used cocaine and coffee and nicotine and other stimulants for years to try and keep myself above a certain level so that the demons of depression would not reach me. My sister and I had an agreement that we would survive no matter what, and I was determined to make good on this agreement.

During this period of my life in New York, I became very involved in the AIDS epidemic while working at the Gay Men's Health Crisis. I started out as a volunteer on their hotline. After attending a support group for a couple of months on Eighthteenth Street, I found myself answering phones, trying to help assuage other people's fears about the growing epidemic. Jerry Johnson, who ran the hotline at the time, had cornered me one day as I was leaving my group. "Why don't you answer phones instead of whining?" I was so taken aback by his frankness that I agreed. The next thing I knew I was hosting a cable show, associate-producing it, making educational films, public service announcements, my whole life just opened up. I found a reason to fight. I even started singing in clubs—the Duplex, Upstairs at Rose's Turn, Good Times. I came alive in spite of my illness. Then one by one everyone around me started to die. Joey, Kevin, Rick, Gary, they were dying in droves. It was so horrible. There aren't words to even convey how horrible it was. It was surreal because on top of the fact that they were all dying, there was the fear of being next, a general public who said that we brought it on ourselves, a president who wouldn't even mention the words, and grief.

No amount of coffee seemed to lift my spirits as I helped to bury the dead. My T-cells continued to drop along with my energy until finally that depression I had avoided so vigorously for years with substances closed in on me and planted itself firmly in the center of my being. My answering machine kept picking up messages as I lay in bed listening to them, wondering what was wrong with me, why I couldn't get up and answer the phone, why I wanted to die. I had just painted the living room white and there was a shiny new razor blade on the kitchen counter where I left it. I should just slash my wrists, I thought. I didn't have the energy. I lay in bed and I prayed to a God I didn't understand to please help me, that I was in serious trouble because I knew that if I got up I would get that blade and slash my wrists and I didn't want to die. A voice in my head said "You're sick. You need a doctor." Just then, and I'm not kidding, just then there was a knock on my door and I jumped up and opened it. It was my ex-boyfriend Ed who happened to be sober. We went across town to Beth Israel Hospital and, before long, I was taking what would become a wonder drug for me: Prozac. Say what you want about it but it saved my life. After spending a couple of weeks in Connecticut with friends while waiting for the drug to take effect, I returned to New York a new man. I threw myself all the harder into working.

I still did not have a clear grasp of how my manic-depression was affecting my life. I was possessed with a determination to make a mark on the world. I had decided that I had to become famous. I would become a famous singer or actor. This was my plan and I set out to do this with a vengeance. I was going to be discovered somehow. Now I don't know if you are manic-depressive and reading this or if you know someone who is, but this may sound familiar to you. I was singing in cabarets at the time and working as a producer and I was certain that it was only a matter of time before I would be discovered. Every so often I would meet or work with someone famous and I was sure that this was my big break. This was going to be the chance that put me on top. I would get increasingly more excited and usually I would start to plan a project of some sort, a recording project was my favorite. I would start out with great enthusiasm and I would generate a considerable amount of energy into producing a project and before long my every waking moment would be consumed with the making of an album. In one such occasion, I had found investors and was working night and day only to have the rug pulled out from under me at the last minute. This was typical of many of the schemes that I would involve myself with. They weren't well thought out, or if they were the people involved often didn't have my best interests in mind. In my manic state, my sights were only set on the final outcome and how famous and rich I would be. I never anticipated any difficulties and often when they occurred, I would treat them as if they were nothing or worse ignore them until things came crashing down on my head. Almost always I ended up in a pickle and this would be followed by a depression. Still, I didn't understand that it was a brain chemistry problem. I took it all very personally and considered that the world was out to get me. I believed that there was a God and that he or she did not want me to succeed or be happy. Unless, of course, I was manic. Then I believed I was God and that I could control the weather and had other special powers. Imagine my frustration when I couldn't make something as simple as a compact disc recording manifest on time! (I rationalized that rain was easier to control than things of this dimension.)

I still had to work to pay the bills, so I continued in AIDS service, leaving the Gay Men's Health Crisis to work for another organization in the fall of 1987. Multi-tasking Systems was a non-profit started by Dr. Linda Laubenstien of Larry Kramer's play *The Normal Heart*. She and a colleague had started the business to help their patients with AIDS continue working with the idea that it would help them to stay healthy longer. I was hired to be the director of job development. I had no formal education or experience in the field except that I had worked at an employment agency for a year as a receptionist, but since I was charming and funny and outgoing they gave me a shot at it. My basic job description was to find employment for people living with AIDS. My secondary responsibility was fund-raising. I was on the verge of mania at the time and slowly but surely my energy went off the charts. This time, there was a different result. I didn't go nuts like I had in years past and I began to be successful. I found people work. I raised money. I went to fundraisers where the rich and famous were hanging out, and because during mania I tended to have little fear, I would just walk right up to whoever interested me and ask them for money. They were usually so stunned by my frankness that they said yes. There is also a point during hypo-mania when a person sort of glows and is magnetic. I positively glowed during the year I worked for this company. Everything I touched turned to gold. I found ninety-three people jobs and raised thousands of dollars. I met Henry Kissinger, Bianca Jagger, and Liz Smith—all in the same evening. Then the shit hit the fan again. Seven people, including my boss, died in one week. For a moment I had forgotten where I was working. Then the epidemic reared its ugly head with full force as my best friend, David, my ex-boyfriend Cal, my boss Christopher, my co-worker Carlos, and three others all died of AIDS-related causes. Carlos died of a seizure right in the office. Christopher worked right up until a few days before his death. Life became a battlefield and once again my mood went off the chart into delusion. The company fired the executive director, a woman named Alice King whom I admired and respected, and replaced her with a man whom I felt contempt for. My days at Multi-tasking Systems became numbered immediately as I began to rebel. The thing I have noticed over the years about mania is that as long as things are going my way, it can be a very enjoyable experience. The energy just flows magically from situation to situation which adds to the delusions of grandeur that occur. As soon as a major stress occurs, say for instance someone disagrees with me for any reason at all, then the trouble begins. Anyone who cuts off the energy flow becomes the enemy. So along comes this new executive director who starts telling me how he wants me to do things and whammo! Mania with agitation begins. This is the stage that precedes mania with psychotic delusions. It is the most unpleasant of my experiences with manic-depression. It causes me to say and do things that I would never think to do in a normal mood state. This set up a very unhealthy dynamic at work and before long I found myself unemployed.

It was during this period of my life that I began to enter into manias that would stop short of full-blown psychotic breaks. My theory is that because of my HIV infection and the fatigue that went with it, I didn't have the physical strength to support a full-blown manic episode so I would have shorter ones. These mini-manias were more frequent, and it was during this time that I became very addicted to caffeine again.

I resigned from MTS Inc. and decided to move to San Francisco. A friend had taken me out there on a vacation and I had fallen in love with the city. I was also ready for a change. I was surrounded by death and was certain that my own number would be up soon. Mentally, I was coming undone and figured that if I didn't change my life somehow, then I would probably commit suicide. I had no friends in California and no job prospects, but it didn't matter. It was time for a change and I was going to make one. I sold whatever I couldn't carry, said goodbye to my friends, and flew out west. I had an offer to stay on a couch for a couple of weeks, which I did until I found a job working in a new age shop. Then I found an apartment. Then I met Matthew and a whole new era of my life began. I was about to experience happiness for the first time in my life. We moved back to Provincetown.

When Matthew and I met, I was sober and drug-free, although I was still smoking cigarettes and drinking coffee. Lots of coffee. Caffeine was my drug of choice and I used it to modulate my energy which, due to HIV, was constantly down. I also was suffering from depression a lot in the first years of our relationship so Prozac was often in the mix. The biggest problems would occur in the spring and summer when my energy would increase and I would start to get very hyper. Often I would redecorate the house and this was a topic of discussion amongst our friends. I would paint the living room a different color every day. Once Matt came home and found me rolling underneath a painting. Just lifting it up and rolling underneath it. I was manic, but I think that at this point people found a lot of what I did amusing rather than irritating because there was never any serious intervention at the time. Things did come to a head one particular summer. When I built a wall in the living room (after Matt said that he wanted another room) out of objects in the house. That was the last straw. With a strain in his voice, one of the first of many in our relationship, he begged me to stop painting and decorating the house. I didn't realize that I was suffering from low-level mania. I thought that I was being creative. I was also trying to please my new mate and so naturally, I was hurt by his request. I was so much in love and I wanted nothing more than to please him. I stopped with the interior decorating and decided that I should try to somehow get rich so that I could buy him all the things that he wanted. He wanted a lot of things. Naturally I ended up getting involved in some pretty hair-brained schemes. One of the best of these was producing the musical *Nunsense*. I had a friend in New York who worked for the writer/director of the show and they came to Provincetown for a visit and we went to dinner. The next thing I knew, me and my big mouth start running and I commit myself to producing the show. Now in my mind I'm going to make a ton of money because I'm going to be working with these famous people, and then I will be able to make Matt happy because he's just not happy unless we have money. This is my thought process. It's a typical thought process when I am in mania. I do not consider the work it will take. The possible difficulties. All I can think about is how much fun it will be, how much fame it will bring me to work with these famous people, and what a lot of money we will all make. There's a name for this symptom. It's called grandiosity. Now the funny thing is that over the years I have produced lots of benefits with many famous people but I do not get a big head when it's for charity. Quite the opposite. I don't know why that is. The minute I am making money and it's professional, I go right off the deep end. Needless to say the whole *Nunsense* experience was a nightmare from the very start. I won't get into the particulars but I will say that it involved a lot of personalities and many mistakes on my part. Add the fact that my mood swings were making my decisions and it's a marvel that I lived to tell even this little part of the story. It is only in hindsight that I realize that it was mania once again that caused me to get myself into a situation that was way above my head professionally. My motive was money. This can be an earmark of my mania. When I start to see dollar signs, look out. It means I am heading for trouble.

Naturally, there was a tremendous crash after the whole *Nunsense* mess. I felt like a failure, and I couldn't understand how I had gotten myself into such a situation. My health was beginning to decline around this time. I was having trouble sleeping and the doctor prescribed Trazadone for sleep which also was supposed to have an antidepressant effect since, at this point, I was in a depression again. Matt and I had entered into couples counseling because we were no longer having sex and we often argued about money. I was complaining about the fact that he had shifted all of his attention onto our dog, which he denied, and he was complaining about everything. We were not happy. It was apparent to me that the relationship was over even though I didn't want it to be. I wanted Matt to be the man I had first met in San Francisco, but he had turned into someone who cared only about money and our dog, and I was sick and dying and I was beginning to dislike him very much. I decided that rather than hate his guts, I would leave him and move to San Francisco. I was a little underhanded in the way that I chose to do this. I went on vacation and didn't come back. I called and told him that he should look for a new apartment.

And then I headed into one of the worst manic episodes of my life.

It lasted for two years and slowly built to a fever pitch that would land me in the same hospital where my mother had sought help decades earlier. After arriving in San Francisco and realizing that my relationship, the one that I thought was going to be "the one," was really over. I went on a pot-smoking binge. I was devastated by this relationship ending. Matt and I had worked in couples' therapy to try to make it work but there was just no saving it. There was something else happening at this time that bears noting also. I had begun, reluctantly, taking the new HIV "cocktail" and was beginning to experience a revival in my health. It is my belief that during the eighties the fatigue that I suffered from HIV kept me from experiencing any full-blown manic episodes. Now that I had a working immune system again and increased energy, I began to topple the charts. It happened slowly but surely. I moved back to Provincetown with the hope of reconciling with Matt but all was lost. I was also using drugs again and this was a problem. I knew that I couldn't continue so I decided to return to meetings.

It was the summer of 1999 and I was trying desperately to put myself together once and for all. I was sober and clean, and I had even quit smoking cigarettes. This was a great accomplishment, for they were my first addiction and the hardest thing to let go of. I was back in therapy and Matt and I had remained friends. Things were looking brighter and I was starting to feel happier and happier.

I was hired to work in a shop on Commercial Street, right in the thick of things, and the owners were two wonderful women and the three of us fell in love immediately. Actually, one of them was more like me than the other. I threw myself into working for them and before long we developed a bond. They were impressed with my sales abilities and talents and before long my head began to swell. I also began to consume more and more caffeine. I was beginning to have a mid-life crisis and, while I have always been vain, I was approaching forty and I became obsessed with my looks in a whole new way. I wanted my teeth to be their whitest and I discovered peppermints with caffeine in them. Rather than drinking coffee, which had stained my teeth, I began to eat these newly discovered mints like candy.

It didn't take long before I had a lot more to worry about besides how white my teeth were. I steadily entered into one of the most colorful episodes of mania I had ever experienced. Matt had helped me to get a job working with some very famous people, and before long I was the talk of the town in all of the wrong ways. Things started out okay at first. But I slowly came apart at the seams and when the producers of the show I was working on fired me, I entered into a full-fledged break from reality. It was a familiar thing for me. All of the same delusions—that aliens were landing, that I was Jesus Christ—returned full force, and before long I realized that there was, in fact, something wrong with my brain.

My therapist showed up at my house on a Sunday afternoon, and since it's hard to get an appointment with him in the summer, I knew that something was seriously wrong with me. He sat in my small apartment looking at possible escape routes as he spoke the following words to me. "Your friends are very concerned for you." At this point I was completely agitated and paranoid and I responded with hostility and venom. "If they are so concerned, where the fuck are they?" (At this point, I had dyed all of my body hair bright orange, weighed 165 pounds and would wear little else other than underwear, thinking that I was really attractive.) He explained that all of them had been coming to him and that they were too afraid to come close to me because of my behavior. Then he begged me to get some help. He wanted me to go to a hospital. I knew that he was right, that I needed help, but I was afraid to tell him all of the things that were happening. If I were honest with him about the stuff that was going on, I might be locked up for good. I also wanted to believe that I really was from outer space. The reality that I was seriously mentally ill was just too painful to accept. I wanted to stay in the euphoria of my manic state. Unfortunately, things were unraveling pretty fast and I was becoming a danger to myself and to others and I could see it. I knew that he was right. I agreed to go to the hospital. What I didn't tell him was that I thought that my car was a spaceship that could wash my dirty clothes and that the clock in my living room was actually a close-circuit television camera to a film studio in NYC that would make me a star. These were just two of many delusions I was now suffering from. I figured I had better keep them to myself until I spoke to the psychiatrist at the hospital I was admitting myself to.

Silver Hill Hospital is located in my hometown. I grew up just up the road from its grounds and all of my life I have known of its existence. My mother was a patient there and I was not very surprised to find myself entering its driveway when the time came.

What did surprise me was when the door locked behind me and they took my belt and shoelaces. Not that this hasn't happened before, just that I never thought that Silver Hill had a locked ward. I found myself on it and the first thing they did was treat me like a crazy person. The next thing they did, which I expected since I had been down this road before, was to give me drugs. I was beyond hyper so they gave me some super duper, calm-you-down drugs, Thorazine, I think, and before long I was coming out of my episode.

I wish I could explain to you what it is like to come down from being so high. There are no words to describe it so I will keep it simple. I became suicidally depressed. Within a few days, I began to remember my behavior in Provincetown and I was mortified. *I wanted to die.* Plain and simple. Even though I did eventually return to Provincetown as you will see, and many people were very understanding and forgiving as it was obvious that I was quite ill, I was beyond embarrassment by my condition and could not fathom forgiving myself. I was also nowhere near getting a handle on managing my illness. I didn't even know how sick I was. I really thought that I would take a few pills and things would be fixed, and that would be that. I had no idea that the road to recovery would take three years and countless attempts with medications before finding the right ones.

The first drugs that I tried were Nerotin and Tegrital with Risperdal for my psychotic symptoms. There was a question of how these drugs would interact with my HIV medications. I was very stressed out, and my doctors were perplexed because my HIV meds were all new. (The good news is that, so far, there have been no noticeable side effects.) I did gain fifty pounds in three weeks. For some reason, and I am sure those of you on these meds or others like them will understand this, you get a voracious appetite. By the time I left Silver Hill, I weighed 230 pounds. I was depressed and had difficulty speaking. I was only home for a month when my depression became so profound that I went back to the hospital. Now I was angry as well as depressed. I had it in my mind that it would be an easy thing to fix me. It was becoming apparent that brain chemistry was very much hit or miss. The next drugs to be tried were Topamax and Xyprexa. I gained more weight on the Xyprexa immediately and I refused to take it. It was back to Risperdal, this time only as needed. I was also taking an antidepressant now to try and lift me out of the dark hole I had fallen into.

Slowly and painfully, I began the march towards sanity. I decided at first that it would be okay if I smoked pot while taking my medications. While smoking it often made me paranoid and delusional, I just didn't want to give it up! I didn't want to give up this crutch and I didn't care what my friends in AA thought. I was determined to hold on to some way to get high. I was also smoking about two packs of Marlboro a day and consuming many cups of coffee, trying to constantly modulate my chemistry and fine-tune my mood swings. Anyone who suffers from manic-depression, or even tiredness, can probably identify with this behavior. Eventually, I was able to let go of the pot, with the help of my support system, and I slowly came into balance. There was a real turning point for me though and it bears some attention in my writing.

I always experience my intense difficulties with mania in the summer months. The stimulation of the summer visitors to Provincetown, coupled with my getting a job, usually put me over the top at some point during the summer and I have to increase my medication. The first summer that I was out of the hospital I was particularly sensitive and I went into a manic episode with great rapidity.

My psychiatrist suggested a new drug that had just been introduced to the U.S. market. He recommended it for a number of reasons. One of the main reasons he knew that I would take the drug is that it would not cause the weight gain that Risperdal and Xyprexa had caused. He knew that it would, as a schizophrenia medicine, help to control my psychotic symptoms and give me a better chance of having a somewhat normal summer.

At first I found the drug very sedating and somewhat frustrating and I would become agitated when I took it. After a short time, about a week, I began to get used to it and I started to find it very helpful. It changed my life!

For the first time in years, I could focus and concentrate on my work. I could listen to music and type at the same time. I could do things that I could never do before. The drug is called Geodon, and if you suffer as I do, I recommend that you speak to your doctor and see if it might be of help to you. I have been able to stay on it longer than any other anti-psychotic drug. This has provided me with some extra added benefits. Things like peace, serenity, focus, and concentration that I could never have imagined were possible for someone like me. I now have the ability to follow through with projects. My illness has caused me to leave so much unfinished business in my life. No more! Thanks to advances in modern medicine, I am a part of the human race. I can complete things. No more gibberish for me. And hopefully, not for you either.

Here are some of the things that I have learned in my struggle over the past three years. I hope you find these suggestions helpful.

1. Stop self-medicating. Drugs that are not prescribed cannot be properly regulated. Pot seems especially popular among people like us (I met many people in the hospital and many people since). You never know the strength of what you are getting and it messes with your other medications, and I believe it causes dangerous psychosis for people like us. It interferes with stability. Give it up! If you can't do it alone, go get help.

2. Be careful of drug interactions with other prescription drugs and with over-the-counter medications. Start a relationship with your pharmacist. Also watch how certain foods, especially caffeine and sugar, affect your moods. Become a scientist. Then avoid the things that unbalance you. I have learned the hard way that sugar and caffeine can hurt or help if not used responsibly. If you have a mild drug interaction, eat carbohydrates and drink lots of water. Get medical attention fast if you feel anything more severe is happening.

3. Get lots of support. It is imperative to have a psychiatrist

and a therapist. Do not try and do this alone. Bipolar disorder is a life-threatening and disruptive disorder. Give yourself every possible chance. If you have a substance abuse problem, get professional help. Do not fool around with this illness, you will not win.

4. Take your medications. The primary failure in the treatment of this disorder is that patients stop taking their medications. There are new and improved medications with fewer side effects and yes, some that won't cause you to gain weight. Investigate them and try them. Give yourself a fighting chance. You are worth it.

5. Make a commitment to yourself to not give up. No one can do this work for you. You are all that you have in the fight to save yourself and you have to do the footwork. It will be very hard. This has been the most difficult three years of my life. Make a commitment to fight for your mental well-being and not give up no matter what the setbacks will be, and you will be glad that you did.

6. Share what you have learned with everyone you meet. Pass this information and whatever else you learn on to everyone you can. You will be amazed, as I was, to find out just how many people suffer from our disorder, or something similar, or know someone who does.

EPILOGUE

September 10, 2002

I wanted to end this all by letting you know what my life is like today. I have achieved a much sought after balance in my life. It has taken much trial and error, and above all *patience.* Patience is not the strong suit of the person who suffers primarily from mania, so you can just imagine what a long road it has been. I would like to thank Dr Stephen Vance, Dr. Ari Kisselenko, and most of all Dr. Matthew Ruble for helping me to stay calm, focused and serene through the hell that is my illness. There has to be a way to convey the intense struggle that has occurred in finding this balance, without discouraging others who suffer from taking up or continuing the fight.

I'm sitting at my desk typing this, watching my cat play, enjoying a moment of morning peace. I have just taken 40 milligrams of Geodon and 100 of Tegrital and 150 of Topamax to try to still a severe mania that had been going on for about two weeks now. I take even larger doses at bedtime and I fight to get to sleep, my mind racing. Part of the excitement and trigger I now know is that I am about to complete and publish this book, a major accomplishment. This is, believe it or not, part of the problem, feeding my mania. I have learned that even positive stimulus can be a problem, one of the more frustrating facets of this disorder. I have also learned that Provincetown in the summer can be a very dangerous place for a manic-depressive as severe as myself. The mistake I made was in thinking that because I had these new drugs I would somehow be immune to the stimulus that affect even everyday people. I was wrong and now I am paying a price. The good news is that it is not the kind of drama that I used to go through. Yes, I am very uncomfortable. I have broken up with my partner eight, or is it nine, times in the last month. I keep asking him to leave. He just patiently waits for the mood swing to end. As I return to balance and the drugs bring me back to a normal state of mind, I realize that I haven't been accepting my illness. This was pointed out to me by my therapist and psychiatrist at my last appointments, and I realize that they are right. If I accept that manic depression is really the problem here, I will have to give up the things that caused this latest attack of mania. Things like dancing in clubs. Working a full-time job, in a high-pressure environment. Hell, I can't even ride my bike down Commercial Street when it's crowded. My doctor, a kind and gentle man, pointed out that a lot of normal people have difficulty with downtown after a while. I so want to be a normal person. I had hoped that, with these new drugs which were helping in so many ways, I would be able to go out and do the things that I had seen others doing with no adverse affects. I was mistaken. For me, the results were disastrous. My relationship suffered and I suffered and the worse part is that only another manic-depressive could really understand what it felt like to have the pain in the head, the agitation, the delusions: the you-don't-love-me and the you-all-hate-me episodes. I think you get the picture.

So, next summer, I will try something new. Now I have to get through the winter. Usually we try Prozac when my depression hits. And it will hit. I can't say which day, but it shows up every year.

It's been a week since I wrote the paragraphs above. The medicines are beginning to slowdown my thoughts, but this is a particularly pesky episode of mania. It is very much like the summer of 1999. The biggest difference is that I haven't roller-bladed downtown in my underwear, dyed my hair red and cursed at anyone who gets in my way. It is a very frustrating thing to be mentally ill. I have to tell myself that things are so much better than they have ever been. I am not in the hospital, and I am managing this crisis so much better than I have ever managed the ones in the past. The fact that I can sit at my computer and calmly report all of these things to you are nothing short of miraculous and a testament to modern medicine as well as my tenaciousness. I have survived so much, and I know that I have learned some more valuable lessons this summer. With this newfound knowledge, I will be able to make this year even more comfortable for myself.

I have added Omega 3 fish oil to my regimen at the suggestion of my psychiatrist as an extra, mood-stabilizing agent. When he first suggested that I do this, I thought he was a quack, but I have since learned that there is scientific evidence to support the use of fish oil in manic-depressive patients. I like the fact that it is a natural substance and is also available in food, since I take so many toxic drugs, HIV and otherwise, and I worry about the long-term effects on my liver. I must say that I am noticing a difference in my overall mood with the addition of the oil, and I do not think it is a placebo effect. I have also recently begun taking a drug called Lamictal. It is an anticonvulsant and it is showing great promise with rapid cycling manic depressives like myself. So far the results are impressive.

For the most part, my life is still somewhat of a struggle, but then whose isn't? At least I have found tools that work fairly well at controlling the ups and downs that this disease throws at me and I am getting better and better at identifying the triggers and stresses that set me off. These are the ingredients to a successful and happy life with manic depression. My HIV is managed for the time being and I am blessed with a strong support system and great health care. I am blessed with a partner who personifies the words "unconditional love." When I am at the end of my rope he is always there to show me that I can do more, be more, try harder. He is a truly caring partner and I am blessed to have him in my life.

Three years ago I was a complete mess with no hope. Now, I have a way up and out. I hope that I have inspired some of you to get help. Today, I don't want to be manic or depressed anymore. I want to be balanced. I want to be peaceful. Mania is a trap. You eventually have to come down and as the Laura Nyro song says, "There is no easy way down." By finding mental heath and sanity, I am getting out of the trap. I am free!

BVG